**Love God.
Love People.
Don't Do Dumb Crap.**

Shane L. Bishop

>>>--<<<

Copyright © 2017 by Shane L. Bishop

Love God. Love People. Don't Do Dumb Crap.

By Shane L. Bishop

Printed in the United States of America

ISBN 978-1-5323-6017-6

All rights reserved solely by the author.

>>>--<<<

DEDICATION

This book is dedicated to my grandchildren
Maddox, Elijah, Mabry and Isaac.
I have become their Papa.
They have become my teachers.
May I always be the "Great and Mighty Papa"
in their eyes.

>>>--<<<

Pains Preamble

>>>--<<<

The time between the completion of my last book *Re:Member* in 2013 and the writing of this book has been most jagged. It has been four years, defined by inexpressible joy on one hand and an unanticipated crisis on the other.

Joy
On the joy side, Melissa and I continue our journey together. We are well into our fourth decade together, and it looks like things are going to work out. Like fine wine, our marriage gets better each year (I don't actually drink wine. I am a Diet Coke guy, but I am quite sure Diet Coke does not get better each year, so we will stick to the wine analogy).

Christ Church, where I am senior pastor, continues to grow in mission, size and stature, and it is becoming clear that my association with this exceptional congregation, now in its third decade, will be the defining feature of my vocational life. Not only that, but as I land in my mid-fifties, I feel very much in my pastoral "prime" (making me glad I was not a professional baseball player, where fifty is *post-mortem* twice removed).

My parents are still in good health, and my almost daily breakfasts with Dad and my Sunday lunches with Mom are regular entries into my "things I will never regret" file.

Crisis
On the crisis side, my daughter's divorce was the most difficult feature of our life during this span of time. A part of this collection is working through this unexpected and unprecedented "death" in our family, and certainly gives some of the early essays an introspective turn. In that, I have found that I increasingly write from the perspective of "hope emerging from pain," in part because it is a wholly new vantage point for me, and in part because it resonates so deeply with so many others. Pain is a powerful common language in a fallen world, but somehow as we learn to speak it with others, pain's icy grip on us thaws and loosens just a bit. At least enough to allow us to breathe once again.

Story
This book features a handful of the "greatest hits" from the first two books, but otherwise is comprised of all-new material. Some of the stories that I have told before have some notes attached and have been slightly rewritten. Just as the death, burial, and resurrection of Jesus appear in all four Gospel accounts, I think it's okay if a few of my stories are repeated for good effect in more than one of my books.

>>>--<<<

Likewise, this book is constructed much like the first two books were; as such, it should be regarded as a collection of stories, musings and proverbs, rather than as a single narrative. In short, it reads much more like Acts than like Genesis. If I hope to one day be known for writing the *Great American Novel*, this will not be it.

This book is, plain and simple, a collection of stories. Stories are to the human experience what songs are to an album or what content is to a publication. Stories are the "stuff" that comprise our lives. Stories offer our lives context and color, help us remember, infuse meaning and convey the pain and exhilaration found in the seemingly unremarkable act of day-to-day living.

Stories are the containers into which we pour our lives. Stories allow us to savor memories, mark time and measure growth. Stories are sacred and holy things both born from and unfettered by time and space. Through story we can go places we have never gone, experience things we have never experienced, learn things we have never learned and meet people we have never met. If my stories help connect you with your stories – or better yet, to The Ultimate Story, then this short book has been a noble enterprise!

>>>--<<<

Why?
I wrote this book because I simply have some hopeful things that I would like to share about life, death and life again. I haven't written in four years. You can't write in storms; the ink runs and the wind drives the rain into your eyes. But you can write in the aftermath of storms. From the vantage point of a storm survivor, you write with both the full memory of the tempest and with some debris still scattered around you.

Storms change us. Storms weather us. I have never written from this place before. I have never been in this place before. I had prayed that I would never be in this place. I wrote this before I could no longer remember it.

Hopes
I hope you are engaged, challenged and even healed by this book. I hope you laugh, cry, reflect, draw strength and find your hearts "strangely warmed," to quote the father of Methodism, John Wesley. The honor of being invited to speak into your life is a privilege that I never take for granted.

Perhaps this book will do as well as *Exactly As I Remember It*, or perhaps it will demonstrate that just because your first book was a hit and the second was a flop, it does not mean your third book can't also be a flop. Or another hit. I have no idea how this will turn out, and that is a part of the adventure.

Title
And then there is the title of this book you're now reading. In late 2015, I was somewhat distressed about the state of the world: Both my world and the world encapsulating me. I was going to work every day, but I was also blocking off some time each evening to feel sorry for myself. Some days I even left work early to get a jump on it.

On one particular day, I was thinking about what would collectively be needed to bring healing to my world, my country, my family and my life. To move us toward what we pray when we say, "Thy Kingdom come … on earth, as it is in Heaven."

Then it hit me: We need to love God, love people and 'not do dumb crap! I published the thought to social media, it "took," and the rest is history – or at least is history(ish).

Ready?
Why not dive into the deep water first? I think I will start at the deep end and swim my way to the shallows. So if you're as ready as I am, then let's begin. With death. Death shouldn't always be placed at the end; sometimes it is the beginning of

new and wonderful understandings and insights. Christians should understand this reality better than anyone. Life for many came only after the death of the One.

Are you ready to begin? It is decided then.

Death is a good place to start an adventure.

No one expects that.

Death and Resurrection

An Opening Reflection

I had a short discussion with an old friend tonight after church. His family is facing some ongoing challenges. He shared what was going on and I prayed with him – on the spot. Upon conclusion, I asked if there was anything else I could do. He said, ""No, just knowing you care is enough.""

I do care … deeply. Often more than anyone can imagine. There are many things that bind human souls to each other in this fallen world. The fact that life sometimes kicks the crap out of us is among them. Perhaps that collective pressure is necessary for the catharsis itself, and if so, pain becomes a precious … even a sacred thing.

Life hurts sometimes. But still we hope and pray and care and share and love and hope some more. Shared pain is a radically egalitarian plane upon which we stand that exposes our need for God and for one another. Shared pain both humbles and unites us; proving that the simple graces of warm empathy and human compassion are most powerful things.

It was, in fact, the pain of One that has offered salvation to all.

Does Everything Happen for a Reason?

There is this idea in popular Christianity that "everything happens for a reason." While I think everything that happens is redeemable, I am not at all sure everything happens for a divine reason. In fact, I am quite sure the reason some things happen is because people do dumb crap. I do, however, firmly believe in a God who loves us, weeps with us, and offers us a living hope that someday death will be swallowed whole by life; that justice will flow like a fountain; and that only faith, hope and love will remain. And on that day God will not say, "I told you so." He will say, "I love you.

Shade in the Valley of the Shadow

This afternoon I was a parish pastor. Nothing more. Nothing less.

Not so long ago, I sat in a nursing home with a friend who, apart from a miracle, would soon die. As we sat together, his wife and I talked. She cried and I cried. He could not talk. He could not cry. He just breathed. There was no leftover energy in him for thinking, talking or crying. Breathing took everything he had.

The two of us listened to him breathe, and in an extended moment of silence, I thought about the impact he had made upon my life. It was significant. She told me of the impact that I had made upon him; it was significant as well. The moment was somehow both holy and humane and thoroughly good. The valley of the shadow of death is funny that way. Shadow sometimes serves as shade ... and in that shade, two weary souls rested and remembered and gave thanks.

I love to preach and lead at the scale God has granted to me, but there are times – sacred times – when just being a parish minister is a wonderful thing.

Today was such a time.

>>>--<<<

P.S. I received a call this evening. My friend emerged from the shadows and leapt into the arms of Christ. It is well. Peace, Jerry. Peace.

>>>>> Believing in the goodness of God is impossible until the pain of your own story gets swallowed up in the victory of a larger narrative. We call that larger narrative resurrection! <<<<<

Moving On (is Really Hard)
Death hurts. Death was not part of God's original plan for humanity, and it remains the tell-tale symptom of a fallen world. When the Kingdom comes, death will have to go. Death must be mourned and mourning can take a while. And the more you had invested in whomever or whatever died, the longer that mourning is going to take. Lots of things die besides people; dreams, physical health, pets, businesses, marriages, careers, mental capacities and friendships can all die ... and each constitutes a very real death.

Some people can't move past a death because they have not yet done the hard work of grieving. Hurt is like dirt: it doesn't go away just because you sweep it under the carpet. The greater the hurt or the longer the dirt has been under the carpet, the greater the chances that you will need some professional help in dealing with it. But that is okay; professional cleaners have equipment that regular folks do not possess.

What is not okay is failing to deal with your issues, because this failure will rob you of the simple gift of enjoying what remains of your life. I encourage you to hold on tightly to hope on one hand, and to let go of dead things on the other. There is life on the other side of death. The resurrection didn't just happen; it is still happening.

A Prayer For Grieving And Hurting Friends

Almighty God, in the pain of these difficult days we have found you once again to be faithful. We have walked through the valley of the shadow and felt its chill, but we did not walk alone.

Be with all who are dealing with catastrophic loss, suffering and pain on this day. Let them know they are loved, and that we – and You – weep with them.

May the mourning be comforted, the grieving find solace, the desperate find hope and the hurting know your healing touch. Give to your beloved ones rest, renewal, revival and restoration. Re-member us, for we have been dis-membered. We can't walk this road without you...
and we are so glad we will never have to.

In Jesus' strong name, Amen !

>>>--<<<

It's About Time

I was thinking about time tonight. Not like Einstein thought about time, but rather, the way that regular people do. Another dear friend suddenly lost his father. What was first an anomaly is now a regular occurrence: my friends are losing their fathers. Time is definitely on my mind.

The New Testament has two concepts of time; chronos, or "chronological time," and kairos or "God time." The former is about quantity, the latter is about quality. Both are gifts. Both come with an expiration date not clearly marked on the packaging. And that is the thing that weighs upon my mind: the expiration date.

We will die. Straight up. And since the clock is ticking; time must be of the essence. Clearly we do not have time to live cautiously, love selfishly, hate bitterly or forgive sparingly. There is simply no time for such shortsighted things. There is an end game we must keep in mind, which is why there is no time to take things for granted. What and who is beautiful, noble and good in your life must be treasured and valued, for it will not forever be. Time guarantees that reality.

Make time for the most important people in your life. You know, those people so important to you that you often take them for granted (while you give your time to people who don't care about you at all). Say, "I love you," send a note, post a pic, drop by, or actually make a call on your phone (do phones still do that?). Tell your precious ones "thank you, I am thinking of you and I appreciate you." Surely you can find time for that!

And then there is the God thing. The one thing in this present darkness that transcends time and blurs death. Make sure you are good there. We only get one shot at getting the God thing right. One.

Tomorrow morning I will eat breakfast with my dad. We will go to McDonald's and eat those horrible little sausage burritos that cost a buck or so, drink about seven Diet Cokes each, and he will tell me all about people I don't know and recount familiar stories that happened forty years ago. He will say, "I know I have told you this story before," and then he will tell it yet again. Then he will ask about how the church is going. And if I am fully awake by then, we will talk for a while.

We are scheduled to meet at 8 a.m., and I assure you ... I will be right on time!

>>>--<<<

>>>>> **It is precisely because we can trust God in life that we can trust God in death.** <<<<<

Emerging from Despair

Tonight I am thinking about my faith journey over the handful of years since my daughter's divorce. I am pondering the subsequent upheaval that engulfed my world like flames. Many knew nothing of what we were going through.

Melissa and I knew it all too well.

In response to the pain I felt each day, I narrowed my world to what I could handle; specifically, to the one mile between Christ Church and our home. I almost completely stopped all outside speaking, consulting and writing. I honestly didn't feel like I had much of anything to say. I went to work every morning and came home every evening to feel sorry for myself. Some days I even left work early to get a jump on it. I loved our lives. Our lives would never be the same again. I just hurt. Melissa hurt. Every single day.

>>>--<<<

Who was I?

I must say that for a while, "it was not well with my soul." The pain and shame of dashed dreams, uncertain realities, and inward fears was overwhelming, as upheavals I never requested or imagined ravaged my soul. "Dear God ... anything but my family."

And yet every Sunday, I declared the goodness of God and preached this wonderful Gospel of a Christ who heals broken hearts; silently praying God would heal the hearts of Melissa and me and of our children and grandchildren.

As I look back from the safe distance of a "new normal" – on this side of the soul tsunami – I find, to my surprise, that there are sunny days again. And even exceptional days, like today, when the world is a snow globe and the shaking of it produces unexpectedly beautiful and wondrous things. I dare to smile again ... and hope ... and dream ... and breathe. Breathe!

By my own estimation, I have emerged from the shadow somehow more humane, forgiving, empathetic, decent, approachable, humble and well ... Christian. I am not damaged. Not permanently anyway. Only things like unforgiveness, bitterness, anger and hate can permanently damage us. I have chosen love and have chosen well, even as I am reminded again (for the first time) that my rightness with God is based on the work *of* Christ, not on my work *for* Christ. And my ministry is based upon the permanence of God's call, not some temporary, illusionary and unsustainable perfection once represented by a "picture-perfect" family photo.

If you are traveling a rough stretch of highway, fear not. The journey may be jolting, but the pain need not be wasted. Through the hurt, devastation and disappointment, you may find that God's work is being done in you and that someday, somehow, quite inexplicably, you will be better for it.
Peace be unto you dear friends, whether you are walking through the valley of the shadow of disease, divorce, hopelessness, rejection, bankruptcy, vocational uncertainty, addiction, loneliness, estrangement or death itself. None of these things can separate us from the love of God. None of these things!

This relentless, forgiving, loving God who has brought you safely this far, will walk with you the rest of the way. The sun will break through. The shadows will disappear. That is the promise. That is enough.

I have now walked through faith, shadow and faith again. My footprints join those of so many of you. Many have walked this road. But know God is for us and not against us. Of this I am certain.
I wasn't, but now I am.

>>>>> Mourning is a type of prayer in which our illusions of control are painfully exorcised from us. Jesus said we are blessed by mourning, for in it we will be comforted. <<<<<

We Christians are a Stubborn Lot

These days I open funeral services – particularly difficult ones – with these words:

> *At the bedrock of our Christian tradition lies a single story. Jesus Christ was crucified, dead and placed in a tomb. And in that moment, it seemed as if evil had triumphed over good; death over life; and despair over hope. Then Friday passed ... and Saturday passed ... but on the third day, on the third day Christ arose.*
>
> *Today we gather to mourn the loss of a dear friend, but we also stand together with the saints in an act of holy defiance. Words like disease, despair, addiction, lost-ness and death do not get the last word, for though a body lies before us, a living soul dances before the Father, singing songs of Zion. That is our story, and it is in celebration of that story that we gather on this day to celebrate life and life eternal.*

We Christians are a stubborn lot, are we not? We refuse to let death have the last word! It is one of the things I like best about us.

Hold on to your faith. Tightly. When we lose faith, we lose everything.

>>>--<<<

>>>>> We all have to traverse tough stretches of highway. Some can be avoided. Some can't.

Some are our fault. Some just happen.
While traveling such roads, get your head up, keep hope alive and remember that God has a wonderful plan for your life.

This rough stretch of highway will not define you. It *must not* define you. Refuse it!
Many have previously traversed your present location and will offer witness that things get better ahead ... much better! Be encouraged! Keep moving forward!

God will never leave you or forsake you. He wouldn't even know how. <<<<<

>>>--<<<

It's Tough Down Here

I couldn't sleep tonight. Never can on Sunday evenings.
Could be I am still jazzed from church.
Could be I am too tired to sleep.
Could be I start my nightly workouts at 10 p.m.
Could be I had four Diet Cokes for supper.
Could be all four.

I was thinking about control, or at least the illusion of it. I am 55 years old. Not yet old, but old-ish. Certainly not young. And I have seen some things on my journey. Most were good. Some were beautiful. Some were terrible.

I have seen people die suddenly, and I have seen people die slowly. I have seen people cut their own lives short, and I have seen dying people fight to live longer still. I have seen love blossom, love promised, love consummated and love blown to crap. I have seen people accomplish great things and lose it all, only to unravel into a happier life than they had before. I have made friends, become cross-threaded with friends, and held some friendships for life. I have seen mended hearts broken, broken hearts mended and broken hearts that refuse to mend.

>>>--<<<

I have discovered that control is an illusion. We can minimize risk, but we cannot eradicate it … there are too many variables.

I truly wish this world was not fallen. I wish all stories ended happily ever, all dreams came true, the people we loved didn't die, and all children grew up nurtured, happy and healthy. But that is the next world; not our own. It's tough down here. And some days it seems tougher than we can bear.

So each day that we awaken, we are faced with a simple choice: we can love, be happy, forgive and hope; or we can hate and be miserable, bitter and hopeless. It is our call. It seems wrong that you have to fight for the good stuff but just because something must be fought for, does not mean it is unobtainable. Even in a fallen world. And choosing to fight for the good in life is really the only thing within our control.

On our last trip to the mountains, I saw this tree. It is not pristine or straight or tall, and I would guess it is seldom photographed. It grew straight for about six feet, took a hard left turn for about five feet and then grew straight again. Clearly its life had once been filled with obstacles and setbacks, but it has chosen to live, to battle, to survive. Over the years, the things that precipitated its turns and twists have disappeared, leaving only a unique tree

>>>--<<<

that chose life. Though it bears scars, its life is clearly better now. Much better. It is a survivor.

From my current perspective, life seems more finite than it once did. Honestly, a bit darker. There have been unanticipated twists and turns but life is good. Really good.

I know now that you don't fall into a good life, stumble into it or luck into it; you choose it. Every single day.

You awaken and you choose. Choose well.

Friendship is less about having answers than having the courage to walk with people in the "valley of the shadow of death."

In this raw valley, pat answers, pithy placards, and trite religious axioms make you wretch, and clichés become obscenities. They are not lies, but neither do they hold true.

Traversing the valley of the shadow is not a soul trek for the fainthearted. Experts are seldom helpful in this valley, but guides are. Guides with warm hearts, a gritty tenacity and an honest and resilient faith – who are willing to walk the difficult trails … and willing to allow hurting people to walk with them.

>>>--<<<

Few churches will ever suffer such a mighty blow ... much less survive it.

Adios and 'Gratchets'
(San Pedro Sula, Honduras, circa 2005)

When we decided to focus a part of the "around the world" ministry of Christ Church in San Pedro Sula, Honduras, I was excited. My dad, also a pastor, had been a part of a mighty movement of God there, and the city was in my blood. After I had made a couple of trips with his No Greater Love Ministries, 2005 was our first official Christ Church trip.

In the weeks leading up to our departure, our 72-year-old Pastor of Visitation, Rev. Ralph Philippe, informed me that he wanted to join the expedition, but I was less than enthusiastic about the notion.

"Ralph, you are older than six kinds of dirt and I can't imagine one good thing that could happen," I told him.

His face turned red, his ears turned purple, and he retorted, "I didn't need a mother before I met you and I don't need one now."

>>>--<<<

When I asked if he knew any Spanish he smiled and replied, *Adios* and "*Gratchets*." Perfect. I had a roommate.

About half way through our trip, Marvin and Karen Steinke, our leaders, split us up into two groups: a medical mission traveling to Tela, on the coast, and a construction crew to stay in San Pedro Sula. I opted for the medical mission and encouraged Ralph to come with me.

"I am not going to do it. I know how to do carpentry, and if I were on the medical mission I would be as useless as you are going to be." We laughed and parted company.

While in Tela, I received word that Ralph had fallen off the roof of the church that his team was repairing. He had suffered serious head injuries and was in a coma. To make a really long story short, Reverend Ralph eventually died from the injuries he sustained on that trip.

Words cannot describe the depths of pain his injury and subsequent death brought to Christ Church.

Words cannot describe how much I miss him.

>>>--<<<

Every now and then I will still run into somebody who knew Ralph and they will inquire if he is still alive.

When I respond, "No," they always ask, "How did he die?"

I reply, "He died well."

The Hope in an Oak

One winter day, I saw an oak tree. It stands not far from my front door. I pass it every day – sometimes five or six times a day – but today I truly saw it. I saw it for the first time. The tree was facing the bright sun on a cold day; warming itself, it seemed. There it stood; humbled by winter, stripped of its leaves but standing proudly … even majestically. It stood straight and muscular, unapologetically and tall; firmly planted in the hope of buds soon to come, green leaves forming, spring rains and warmer days. The hope of warmer days … it sounds wonderful, doesn't it?

This event in my early pastoral ministry literally devastated me ... in all the ways I most needed devastated.

Deferred
(Giant City, Illinois, circa 1994)

When God called me into ordained ministry in the spring of 1989, it changed the trajectory of my life. By the fall I was enrolled in seminary and had moved Melissa and the kids halfway across the country and away from parents and grandparents in Southern Illinois (which now seems unthinkable). Three years later, we moved back to Illinois and had served under appointment in Sumner for a couple of years.

I was preparing to undergo my final step toward Elder's orders in the United Methodist Church. With probationary time served, seminary graduated with honors, psychological taken and paperwork complete, all that stood between me and final ordination was a perfunctory interview with a small group of Elders. I had every reason to think things would go well. I had been informed of no problems during my probationary period, my counseling elder was fully supportive of me, my District Superintendent seemed high on me, and my two churches were thriving. But that is what you get for thinking ...

>>>--<<<

The interview was held at Little Grassy Campgrounds outside of Carbondale, and I was ready to celebrate. Dinner reservations had been made, the families had been invited and I was honestly expecting a lot of affirmation. It was going to be the best day of my life!

To say the interview went poorly would be an understatement. I was blindsided and left rejected, stunned and devastated. I was invited to come back the next year, after I had jumped through a few more hoops. Unlikely.

For a full year the deferment defined me; that interview played a million times in my head and the pain bled into every area of my life, family and ministry. It was not well with my soul. Not well at all.

Then there was the night I decided to leave the United Methodist Church. It was about nine o'clock in the evening and the decision was finalized in my heart, when the phone rang. Melissa handed the phone to me (in the bathtub) and told me that Rev. Dwight Jones was on the other end. Dwight was a well-respected pastor; he had never called before, and I really didn't know him all that well.

>>>--<<<

"Shane, I don't really know why I am calling, but I felt I should tell you to not give up, and that God has big plans for you in the United Methodist Church." Dwight went on for a while encouraging me, told me about his own deferment, then hung up, completely unaware of the pivotal role that that single call would play in my life.

After sitting out the ordination process in 1995 (I was still in a bad mood), I went back before the Board of Ordained Ministries in 1996 and received the kind of treatment I had anticipated two years earlier. I was passed through with flying colors, chosen to represent my class in taking the flame from retiring Elder Dr. Paul Simms, and was awarded the Harry S. Denman Award for effective evangelism. My ordination was a good day. A really good day.

Through that season of my life, I learned a lesson I will never forget: Good times do not make up for bad times; they are just good. God has blessed me with more success in ministry that I could have ever imagined back then, but the pain of that experience never quite goes away. I find it fascinating that the resurrected Christ still had scars. He showed them to Thomas! I have scars as well. So do you.

Death always leaves a mark.

>>>--<<<

It has left a mark on me. It has left a mark on you.

I am better for it. I hope you are as well.

And if you are not yet well; I hope you will be, one day … I truly do.

>>>--<<<

Scars and All

I recently drove along a gravel road near Townsend, Tennessee, that was once a railroad track bed. The wooded area called Tremont is beautiful, with a stream running through it that jumps from one side of the raised road to the other. I paid my dollar and picked up an auto guide that relayed a story that was difficult to believe.

About 100 years ago about two thirds of the present Great Smoky Mountains National Park was clear cut. The pictures from that time are stark and unbelievable. Loggers pulled down the trees, great steam machines loaded massive trunks onto box cars, and geared steam engines pushed the cars about four or five miles to a sawmill, a few hundred yards from my (not-five-star) motel.

Workers and families lived in 12-by-12 portable shelters that lined the railroad tracks, giving rise to names like *Stringtown*. The modest homes rented for one dollar per month. Erosion ravaged the picked-bare mountains and sparks from steam engines ignited forest fires that burned for days or weeks.

Then one day the area became a national park. The loggers left, the hotel closed; the saw-mill cut its

>>>--<<<

last board in 1938. What was left behind was a veritable disaster.

Then there was a long slumber as the land was given time to heal. Decade after decade, the land healed. Now, some 75 years later, you would never believe the desolation that now can only be verified by photographs and scars that are barely discernible, and only if you know where to look: A pipe just rising above the ground here; a braided metal wire there, buried in a tree with its origin in a rock. The casual observer would not see these scars, they would see only splendor. These mountains are healed.

I know a lot of Tremont-type people. They are people with old scars and deep pain that have somehow healed, mended, and softened over time. To look at these folks today, their lives would not even hint at their troubled pasts for they have become pristine, beautiful and are again made whole.

Healing a person, like healing a forest, takes time, intentionality and care. Such healings are a compelling testimony to a loving and restoring God.

That is why our personal stories of restoration and healing must be shared … scars and all.

>>>--<<<

The 'God is Good' Story
(Sumner, Illinois, circa 1996)

Sometime in late 1992, I attended a seminar in Peoria, Illinois on how to do ministry with senior adults. This ancient, feeble man inched up to the platform (like Tim Conway used to do on the "Carol Burnet Show") and opened the thing up by proclaiming, weakly: "God is Good." The people replied, "All the time!" He quietly responded, "All the time," and they politely finished, "God is Good."

I remember thinking to myself, "This is almost cool! I wonder what would happen if *living* people tried it?"

The potential of this greeting captivated me, and all I could think about was putting a V-10 engine and glass packs on this thing and flooring it the very next week at my service in Sumner. Our first four or five tries the next Sunday morning were a little lame, but after that, "God is good!" became an institution. Every worship service I conducted at the Sumner United Methodist Church began with a rousing, "God is good!" It was a bold and upbeat way to begin our worship services ... until that exceptionally cold winter.

>>>--<<<

It was Advent, 1996. Advent in the United Methodist world is a traditional time of preparing our hearts for the arrival of the Christ Child on Christmas. On Wednesday, Melissa had been informed that our third child, a son whom we were to call Liam, had died in her womb. Nothing could be done until the next week, and Sunday loomed in between. We were devastated. It was as if the best Christmas present in the world had been placed under the tree – only to be snatched away in a cruel cosmic joke. Never had I felt so crushed, staggered and utterly ... de-converted.

All I could think about was the expectation that I would start that next worship service with "God is Good!" I had no idea how I would do that. Never had I less perceived God to be good than in that moment, and the prospect of proclaiming it was more than my weary heart could bear.

These were the days before hospital privacy laws existed, so everyone in our "one-Casey's town" (though we were yet to actually get a Casey's) knew what was happening. Rural folks know well how to dance with pain and death, so they gave us space to hurt, and when we walked into the church, folks steered clear.

Our names were printed on the bulletin: Melissa Bishop, followed by Shane Bishop. Melissa, along

>>>--<<<

with her best friend Sherri Baker, were scheduled to open by singing a song called "Harmony," about God's gift to creation of a baby boy. It seemed … ironic. I was to follow with a rousing, "God is good!" I could not possibly imagine how any of that was going to happen.

To my amazement, when the prelude concluded, Melissa (with our dead baby in her stomach) quietly arose from her seat, and in beautiful harmony, sang of a baby's arrival long ago. My stolid congregation listened with quivering lips, fighting back uncharacteristic tears as they marveled at the Spirit-energy of this incredible woman, temporarily caught between a rock and a holy place.

As I sat in awe of Melissa's inner strength and the sheer power of her spirit, something occurred to me. If God is not good at this very minute – I mean "right now" – then He wasn't good last week and wouldn't be good a month from now. It was as if God spoke to me, saying, "I am either good or I am not good, and you have about thirty seconds to decide." When the song ended, I walked behind that wooden pulpit and shouted for my soul, "God is Good!" to which the people nearly raised the roof as they replied, "All the Time!" I was re-converted.

>>>--<<<

For the past two-and-a-half decades, I have opened each of our worship services with "God is Good!" But never assume that it is always an easy thing. Sometimes you have to fight for it.

Liam would be twenty-one now. There will forever be an empty seat at our table. Melissa and I think of him often. Still ...

>>>--<<<

A Beautiful Disaster
(Fairview Heights, Illinois, circa 2007)

The center sanctuary window at Christ Church was created by artist Ken vonRoenn. It is huge, round and comprised of four panels. He attended church here a time or two, got our vibe, then created an incredible work of art. The piece was scheduled to be installed on November 27, 2007, as the final touch before the grand opening of our new 1,100-seat sanctuary. We were so excited!

Despite the fact that the window sits about fifty feet in the air, the first three panels were installed without incident. But late in the evening, the unthinkable happened. While the installers were on top of the scaffolding, we had a brief electrical blackout. The panicked installers couldn't see where to set the glass; as a result, it hit the scaffolding, hard. The glass remained in place, but the design within the pane had shattered. They hurriedly took the final panel down, loaded it up and sped back to the studio in Kentucky.

We opened the new sanctuary with just three-quarters of an art window. It was a disaster.

One day we received a call from Ken, who suggested that rather than create a new panel of glass (which would be impossible to match), that

>>>--<<<

we shatter the other panels as well. I was suspicious at best, until I saw it. The shattered pane was … beautiful! It was infinitely more interesting and complex than it had been before, and with our approval, the artist made short work of shattering the other three panes of glass.

The central feature of our 1,100-seat sanctuary is a beautiful disaster! Our shattered window stands as a witness to the restorative power of God.

A Prayer of Death and Life

Almighty God, be with those who are experiencing new beginnings and with those dealing with difficult endings on this day.

Bless those whose hearts are light and those whose hearts are filled with pain.
Make us all ever more willing to dance with those who dance and weep with those who weep – and remind us that in both of those times, and in all times in between – you are God.

Help us to so respect you that we can respect ourselves, and so respect ourselves that we can respect others.
Give us grace to forgive ourselves that we may forgive others and to so love you that you may love others through us.
And in the laughter and tears that this day inevitably will bring, remind us that our hope is not in our grip upon You but in Your grip upon us.

In the strong name of Jesus, Amen!

>>>--<<<

Life Hacks

Musings on My Roaring Mid-Fifties: Wine and Diet Coke

I was a part of the DuQuoin High School class of 1980. I am now 55. If I live to be 110, I am currently middle aged.

Here some of the ups and downs (and downs and ups) I have discovered from this season of life:

1. **Down:** What of my hair is not turning gray is jumping ship.
Up: I really don't care very much.

What makes us who we are is far deeper than appearance. That being said, I wish I appeared to have more hair.

2. **Up:** My proverbial skin is thicker.
Down: My literal skin has stuff that has to be burned off it each year.

It is a good thing to not be worried about criticism 364 days a year. The dermatologist's blowtorch to the epidermis on day 365, however, is rough.

3. **Up:** I am established.
Down: I must not become establishment.

>>>--<<<

The second you lose the fire in your belly is the second your best days are behind you. You have to stay hungry!

4. **Down:** I have lost a step ... or two.
Up: You see a lot of things you used to miss when you lose a step or two.

You can't smell the roses at a 24-7-365 all-out sprint. And not only that, slowing down means you must get more efficient and smarter to compensate.

5. **Down:** The demands upon my time are immense.
Up: Since I can't do everything and can't be everywhere, more great people have come alongside of me.

I am mortal. It is inconvenient. One is too limited a number to accomplish very much at all. How we spend our time and on whom we invest our time are the most important decisions of this season.

6. **Down:** There have been disappointments.
Up: Disappointment has made me keenly appreciative of what I do have.

When you realize you deserve nothing, you begin to appreciate everything! Thanksgiving is the antidote to entitlement.

7. **Down:** I recognize my mortality.
Up: I have tapped into a humaneness that guides every aspect of my life.

Realizing we don't have all the time in the world, makes finishing well an ever more important goal. People with less money must invest what they have more wisely; it works the same with time.

8. **Up:** Wine improves with age.
Down: Diet Coke does not.

Middle-age is really not all that bad. There is actually symmetry and even kindness to it. For example, the second you begin to look older, your eyesight begins to dim.

Keep smiling.

Keep loving.

Keep growing.

Keep faith alive.

>>>--<<<

Musings on Respect

I don't think there is a more attractive virtue in this divided country than respect. People have always told me that "respect must be earned," but frankly, I disagree. I only know a couple hundred people well enough that they have had a chance to earn my respect, so if everyone has to earn it, I am not going to respect most of the people on the planet.

Here is a radical idea: Let's offer everyone respect, and make people earn disrespect. Certainly, there are people who have, by their own actions and attitudes, earned my disrespect – but why not offer the other folks the benefit of the doubt? What if we all made respect and not disrespect our default toward others?

I have long maintained that if you want to see someone's true character, pay attention to how they treat people who could never do anything for them. Everyone treats powerful people well (to their faces anyway) but what about the people who could never upwardly network you or give you a raise or a promotion? What if we treated everyone– I mean everyone – equally well? And really well!

This week, I encourage you to be respectful in what you say, how you act, what you post and what you tweet. Retreat to "out-of-fashion" virtues like calling people "sir" or "ma'am. Say "please" and "thank you." Extend the gift of the benefit of the doubt. Show the person working the counter at McDonald's the same kind of respect you would your boss' boss. I have discovered that people tend to act significantly more respectful to others when they are shown respect by others. Respect is actually quite contagious; it can even go viral! There is simply no downside to treating people really well.

You want to change the world? Here is a place to start: Open the door for someone who has their hands full and give them a warm "you are most welcome," when they thank you. I assure you, that is a door that swings both ways.

Life Hacks Collection No. 1

- There is no more lame excuse than "I can't find the time." We all have the exact amount of time. 24 hours. Every day.
- Only if an idea sounds as good in thirty days as it did the second you thought of it, is a good idea.
- Believe none of what you hear and only half of what you see ... no down side here.
- Think about the life you want to have in five years. Are the decisions you are making today taking you toward that life? Repeat that question again tomorrow.
- You can't live forward by looking backwards.
- We don't forgive to let those who hurt us off the hook; we forgive to break their power over us.
- Be suspicious of your doubts.
- Leadership decisions are never universally popular. Universally popular decisions do not require leadership decisions.
- Most things resolve themselves without intervention. Some things don't. The hack is to recognize the difference.

Down Cycles

I define down cycles as the rough stretches of highway that life sometimes tosses at us. Down cycles consistently have you making decisions out of a distorted position of weakness, rather than from a clear position of strength. Such decisions are almost always impulsive, and consistently yield poor results in the long run.

Learn to associate down cycles with holding steady; with not quitting your job, not getting a divorce, not spending your life's savings on lottery tickets, not changing religions, or not buying a new house.

Down cycles are like thunderstorms: they can hit hard (and it can hail), but they don't usually last very long. And when they pass, the atmosphere is stabilized (at least for a while). Control the impulse. Hold course. Pray through. Save the big decisions for another time.

>>>--<<<

This story seemingly applies to all situations in which someone expects you to do what they are not doing themselves. So to say the least, I think of it often.

What You Can't Do in an Hour a Week *(Manchester, Georgia, circa 1991)*

Something remarkable happened during my three years in seminary at Candler School of Theology at Emory University in Atlanta: we had a really good life. Lydia was just a baby and Zec started kindergarten our first year there.

1990 was Zec's first year of organized baseball, and in Manchester, where we lived, baseball was highly organized. The league was called "Dixie Youth," and the teams were named after professional franchises. When the powers-that-be discovered I had been a former baseball coach, they gave me Zec's team to manage: the Yankees. Being from Illinois, everyone thought this was hilarious that I was the Yankees' coach, and perhaps it was.

In my final season before we moved back to Illinois, I had a situation that threatened to ruin my summer. It was the year the kids moved from coaches pitching to them to facing "live" pitching -— not that the coaches are dead. This was a

{51}

game-changer for many of the boys, as a large percentage of eight-year-olds don't have pinpoint control, and a small percentage of eight-year-olds can throw really hard.

I had a really nice kid on my team who was, simply put, a terrible baseball player. He showed up on the first day of practice with a new set of batting gloves, a new fielder's glove and a new bat. My initial observation that none of these pieces of equipment had ever been used was not lost on me.

As the season progressed, it became clear this kid was never going to have any success in baseball whatsoever, and the boys began to dread his at-bats because they were always sure outs. In close games, it always seemed his one at-bat a game, required by the rules, came when we had two outs and runners in scoring position.

Sometimes I hoped this kid would get lucky, get hit by a ball, and actually get to go to first base one time before the season ended, but he had no such luck (despite an obvious lack of hand-eye coordination, he had pretty quick reflexes for avoiding errant baseballs.)

One day after a late-season game, his dad, more than a bit agitated, approached me.

>>>--<<<

"Coach, why are you not playing my son as much as the other boys?" He went on, turning up the intensity. "I bought him a new glove, a new bat and a new set of batting gloves and he isn't even getting to use them."

Finally, I had had enough – I get that way after a while – and responded calmly, "Sir, I don't play your son because he is a danger to himself when he is on the field. Some of these boys can hit, and he does not even catch well enough to protect himself. On top of that, he can't even begin to hit. If you think it is building his self-esteem to be placed in a position every week where he cannot possibly succeed, you are dead wrong."

The father, a bit deflated now, responded defensively, "Coach, it is your job to teach him to play baseball."

I retorted, "You are wrong again, sir. I only have these kids for an hour in practice and a game each week. The boys who are good at this age, are good because their parents spend time with them teaching them how to catch, throw and hit. You have not done these things with him, and buying him new equipment will not replace the hours it takes to develop these skills.

"I cannot do for your child in an hour a week what you have failed to do over the past nine years of his life."

Truth.

>>>>> You will never make yourself look better by trying to make someone else look bad.
Take comfort in knowing many people can look plenty bad all by themselves.

Take the high road. You seldom get dirty and the view is so much better! <<<<<

>>>--<<<

Don't Punish Success

When I was young, I had freckles. This seemed acceptable because I never had acne and was completely positive that I would never go bald. I remember watching with horror as some of my high school and college friends began to lose their hair and seeing their fathers' hairless craniums left little doubt as to why. I felt sorry for these mates because my dad was blessed (and is still blessed) with a great head of hair, and I was certain that this fine trait had been passed to me.

It all started about five years ago when I thought the top rear region of my skull was flattening. When I felt my head, there was a flat spot and I could not imagine what was happening. Was my head going flat? Was I jamming my head against the headboard as I slept? Did either of my grandpa's have a flat head? What was happening is that my hair was beginning to thin, and things were ever-so-slowly getting out of hand. When I watch videos of me preaching from year to year, it is incontestable that I am losing hair density (and pigment) at an alarming rate.

Earlier this week I happened to pass a mirror. For some reason I noticed a single hair in the thinning back region that was shooting straight out and about an inch longer than the competition.

>>>--<<<

Instinctively, I reached up to pluck it, and then it hit me. What kind of failing business owner punishes his only high performing salesman? What coach benches his best player?

I went into my bathroom, found some scissors, and carefully trimmed the hair to the length of the rest. I even put some gel on it. It was glorious.

I hope the others are inspired!

>>>--<<<

We Are All Full of Something
(And We All Leak)

My first epiphanies upon entering the world of social media – where: people are unhappy, there are a lot of them, and they are happy (pun intended) to post about it.

Clearly, there is something about chronic misery that makes people suddenly want to share bad news with others. The mantra seems to be, "If I am unhappy, you should be unhappy too, and I am going to do my best to help you see the world my way. No need to thank me." We certainly have plenty of angry, hapless, jaded, sardonic and melancholy missionaries in this world! Tragically, most of them have access to a computer.

When I read such calamitous posts there is one thing their authors all seem to have in common: a lack of hope. There seems to be a self-fulfilling pessimism hardwired into their emotional construct that they either can't or don't care to shake. There is this discordant vibe raging through them that says, "Things were bad, things are bad, and things are going to continue to be bad."

Hopeless.

>>>--<<<

Systems Theory simply states that all systems are designed to produce what they produce, not what you desire them to produce. So here is the deal: If you are unhappy with your life, everything in your life is designed to produce that unhappiness. If you want to change your outcomes, you have to change your inputs. I think most people want to be happy; they are just not quite sure how to change their inputs, so they keep entering the same negative stuff into their systems that they have always entered, as that is all they know how to do.

I don't think God went to all the trouble of sending Jesus to Earth and raising him from the dead so we could be miserable. We could have been perfectly miserable without the resurrection. So where is the hope?

I believe the best route to happiness is found by drenching, marinating, and saturating our lives with huge helpings of straight-up hope! My favorite steak in the world is the filet at Andria's Steakhouse in Fairview Heights, Illinois. They choose great pieces of beef, but the trick is in their sauce. They marinate those steaks to the point that every single bite is absolutely delicious. To use one of my favorite double negatives, there is *no way not* to find a delicious bite on a filet at Andria's; it is literally infused with tantalizing hope!

>>>--<<<

Want different system outcomes? Infuse your system inputs in hope!

Some Hope Infusions for Body, Soul, and Spirit!

1. **Increase your exposure to hopeful people.** Watch hopeful and upbeat people. Read what they post online. Note how they interact with others. Hang around these folks all you can!

2. **Decrease your exposure to hopeless people.** If there are people in your life who consistently bring you down, limit their access to you! Unfriend them or hide their posts. Misery is contagious and it is easy to tell who is infected.

3. **Subscribe to sources that breed hope and optimism in you.** Think about the things in your life that give you energy, joy, and fulfillment. Do more of those things.

4. **Unsubscribe from sources that reinforce pessimism.** Think about the things in your life that give you indigestion, cause stress, and make you feel crummy about yourself and the world around you. Do less of these things.

5. **Speak positively.** I believe words are powerful things, and like boomerangs, our words tend to fly back in our direction once launched. Don't set any

words into motion that you wouldn't want coming back at you! Encouraging words are the building blocks of a hopeful world view.

6. **Refrain from speaking negativity.** My mom used to say, "If you can't say something nice, don't say anything at all." That will work.

7. **Decrease your time with media.** I am often perplexed when people complain about the negativity in the media, because media is something we INVITE into our lives. We choose our Facebook friends, what we see on the internet, who we follow on Twitter, and which television stations we watch. Take control. If you can turn it on, you can turn it off.

8. **Increase your time in the Bible.** Stop watching a thirty minute show each day or perusing your Facebook feed, and substitute that time with Bible reading. Start with Matthew, Mark, Luke, John, or Acts. Read the great stories of Genesis. Spend some time in the Psalms. Be inspired!

9. **Stop thinking about yourself.** Hopeless people have very small worlds that get smaller by the day. Their attention is focused on "me and mine" and "us and ours."

>>>--<<<

10. **Start thinking about others.** Hopeful people live in big worlds and are actively making better worlds. Their attention is focused on serving God and serving others.

Each of us is a product of the systemic input we invite into our lives. If you do not like your life, you are the only person who can change it. New outcomes require new inputs. I have often said that "we are all full of something, and we all leak." Why not fill ourselves with hope and let it leak out everywhere?

I saw a young couple on a date while we were at "B Dubs."

**They were staring at their phones.
Heads down.
Thumbs flying.
Neither looked up.
All evening.**

Were they texting each other?

{61}

>>>--<<<

Musings on What We Share in Common

How might the world change if we chose to focus on the one building block that we all share in common: that we are all human beings? DNA experts claim all humans are 99.9 percent the same. They also say we share 50 percent of our DNA with a banana, but I digress.

I find it fascinating that we humans want to look to almost anything to define us, other than our humanity. We seem most comfortable in quickly tossing ourselves into divided groups, and tragically, it is often as a part of these groups that we have our identities. We are Democrats or Republicans, labor or management, married or single, white- or blue-collar, rich or poor. We are red, yellow, black or white; hip hop or country, PhD or GED, conservatives or progressives, PETA or NRA, military or civilian and the list goes on, into infinity.

These days it is as if you meet a person and the first thing you are expected to do is put yourself into a series of categories. "Hi, my name is Shane and I am a married, traditionalist, Methodist, Caucasian, Cardinals fan with two master's degrees who loves history, really likes baseball better than politics and enjoys mid-tempo music with really good lyrics, and if you are different than me on any one of these things, there is a good chance I hate you."

Do you see how different this is than, "Hi, my name is Shane and I am a human being. Can you imagine how much we have in common?"

Pray for the grace to see beyond dividing walls of statistical categories, and to instead view people as human beings. Human beings of sacred worth, lovingly formed and fashioned in the image of our Creator.

You may be shocked to find out we are not all that different after all!

>>>>> There is nothing more intrinsically selfish than allowing yourself to have a bad attitude. You become emotional second-hand smoke carelessly inflicted on everyone who has the misfortune to be around you. Stop it!

People who have great attitudes don't have better circumstances or better dispositions than everyone else. They just work harder! <<<<<

>>>--<<<

The key to success is found in moving the needle each and every day. It is more often a simple discipline than a breakthrough event.

Winning the Day
(Olney, Illinois, circa 2013)

There are few things I enjoy doing more than hanging out with my friend Jim Baker. This isn't the circa 1980s television evangelist Jim Bakker, or James Baker the statesmen. This is just plain Jim Baker. Well not just plain … Jim had a gift for which people still remember him in Lawrence and Richland Counties. Jim could flat-out throw a baseball.

I first met Jim Baker in 1992, and we soon became good friends. Over the years, we have become more like brothers. I remember the first time I caught Jim. He wound up, had a smooth delivery, and the ball literally exploded out of his hand. I played college ball, but had never seen anything like it! After about five horrifying fastballs, he flipped his glove, indicating he was going to throw a breaking ball. I couldn't even swallow. I somehow caught the ball (with eyes closed), jogged to him, placed the ball in his glove, and we have never played catch again.

>>>--<<<

After a great college career, Jim had a brilliant minor league career with the Toronto Blue Jays organization, excelling at every level but never quite making it to The Show.

Jim and his wife Sherri attended the Sumner United Methodist Church, and in the summer of 1992, I became their pastor and they soon became our closest friends. In those days Jim coached and taught history at East Richland High School before jumping into the insurance industry. Though we don't see each other as often these days, Melissa and I treasure our time with Jim and Sherri more than ever (now that we have so little of it).

On this "hotter-than-six-kinds-of-smoke" summer day, Jim and I were taking a walk with Melissa and Sherri, along the oiled-and-chipped lake roads near Olney. We lagged behind them fifty yards or so and initiated our own conversation. As always happens with us, we cleared the catch-up and chit-chat talk quickly and picked up our friendship right where we left off last time. I asked Jim how his spiritual life was going. He literally lit up at this question.

"Really well," he replied with some energy, "I think I have this figured out! I wake up every morning, pray, read the Bible and decide I am going to win the day for the Lord. And then I do the same thing all over again tomorrow."

Then it occurred to me. Just like throwing strikes and staying ahead in the count, Jim has discovered the key to becoming a person of God! You simply have to win the day! And then repeat tomorrow.

>>> 10 Ways to Win the Day <<<

1. Encourage someone
2. Thank someone
3. Reach out to someone who is hurting
4. Dream with someone
5. Pray for someone
6. Invite someone to church
7. Mentor someone
8. Show kindness to someone
9. Forgive someone
10. Show love to someone

Do these things and the "someone" who will have the great day is you!

#PDTP (Put Down the Phone)

I have stopped taking my smartphone everywhere with me of late.

I have clearly made it angry. It has started to slow down and seems passive aggressive as it spins when I ask it to do its job these days.

But the reality is that it doesn't want a job; it wants to control my life. But that is all over. It no longer gets to go to restaurants with me, it does not get to go to meetings with me, and when I am with my family, it does not get to come along. It is often relegated to "do not disturb" mode for hours on end, so even when it comes along, it is not allowed to talk or ring or vibrate or make other siren sounds.

My phone is NOT a family member; it is a phone, and if I threw it in a lake my life would go on just fine. It does not get to interrupt conversations, ring at inappropriate times, or vie for my attention any longer. It will not place me in an OCD trance for hours on end any more.

Relationships have won. My smartphone has lost. Humanity has once again triumphed over machines. Temporarily anyway ... #PDTP

Here is another reason to leave your smartphone behind when you have lunch with actual humans. It takes the fun out of all delightfully petty and irrelevant arguments, by offering instantly accessible and boringly correct information.

Who needs correct information at lunch?!? You only need that at work!

For example, disagreements over who sang "Thunder Island," who backed up Tim McCarver at catcher for the 1967 St. Louis Cardinals, or who Lincoln's third general was should take at least twenty minutes, and parts of the discussion should be heated.
The possibility of later finding out you were right or that you have made a total fool of yourself is an American right we should never give away in the face of technology.

Going to lunch? Leave your phone in the car.
It ruins everything.

>>>--<<<

Drama Intolerance Syndrome
(I Have a Bad Case)

I have DIS. "Drama Intolerance Syndrome" (I might have made this up), and it causes me plenty of *dis-ease*. I find that drama makes me irritable which, of course, only adds to the drama.

I fully realize that in a fallen world populated with humans with internet access, there is going to be SOME drama. I get that. What I can't tolerate is perpetual drama, recreational drama, drama as entertainment and drama evangelists.

Social media is a real challenge for people who lack self-awareness. Some people consistently post things that make them seem needy, weak, imbalanced, pitiful and pathetic – and then they wonder why people think they are needy, weak, imbalanced, pitiful and pathetic. Other people post unbelievably insensitive, rude, uncompassionate or divisive things – then wonder why people think they are insensitive, rude, uncompassionate and divisive.

Here are four quick suggestions on how to decrease some of the drama in your cyber life.

1. If you truly were happier before social media took over the world, disconnect from it now.

Deactivate your account and be done with it. I assure you the cyber world will not miss you (or me) but you may be healthier without it.

2. **Don't be afraid to use the "unfriend" option.** Cyber "friendships" end quite painlessly, and "unfriending" a person who aggravates your DIS with every post will actually be much better for your real-life relationship (if you actually have one). There are LOTS of people I liked better before I knew their every thought. And if they notice you "unfriended" them and ask why, tell them the truth with all kindness.

3. **Be careful with what you post.** Some people post stuff that is sure to cause a firestorm, then honestly can't figure out why they got burned. If you aren't sure you should post something, don't. If you can't take it, don't give it and if you don't want it, don't ask for it. Also if you don't want people in your business, don't hang your dirty laundry in front of their house. Christians today would do well to be quick to pray and slow to post.

4. **Develop a mission statement for your social media use.** "To keep up with friends and family" or to "Help connect people with Jesus" are two examples. And then stay on mission. Don't get drawn into religious arguments, political scrums,

relational drama, or debates you don't want to enter.

By being honest with ourselves, determining what the role of social media should be in our lives, we can enjoy all the benefits of social media, without adding to the macro drama on one hand and without adding micro drama to our lives on the other.

When it comes to posts, tweets and what-not, when you have doubts about whether you should post something ... don't post it. You will never regret the potentially self-damaging and others-damaging things you choose not to post.

My mission is "to celebrate the joy of authentic Christian living." Faith, music, art, sports, history and culture all support this mission; criticism, party line politics, denominational arguments, rancorous debate, personal pontification and dogmatic diatribes do not. I want to keep it positive and have a good time while I am at it.

Social media offers some real opportunities to enhance or detract from the quality of your life. Facing it honestly, intentionally and with a mission will make sure what you hoped to be a blessing doesn't turn into a curse.

>>>--<<<

>>>>> **Saying hurtful things and apologizing is a bit like running over a dog with a truck and apologizing:**

It all feels about the same to the dog. <<<<<

Whatever Helps You Sleep
(circa August 2015)

Maddox begins kindergarten tomorrow. Elijah begins next week. I am surprised at how much this has affected me. It is terrible, really.

Since Maddox and Elijah were born, Fridays have been days with "The Great and Mighty Papa!" Mabry and Isaac soon jumped right in. The second you are potty trained, your Fridays belong to Papa.

Fridays are all about a whirling dervish of chicken nuggets, total disasters (see *Poop-a-Geddon*), special drinks, Monkey Joe's play place, partial disasters, playgrounds and ice cream. I cannot tell you how much I enjoy these Fridays with my grandchildren, and now the game is changing.

>>>--<<<

Doesn't someone have to have my approval to change the game? Time out! I want a replay.

Imagine this: The two boys will be in school an astounding five days a week. Including Fridays! The boys will be with *them* and not *me.* Who needs to go to school five days a week? Will the school people even know that I call Maddox "The Mungon" and Elijah "Lijjie-Man?"

Don't schools know that Friday is water day at Nana's in the summer and McDonald's indoor playgrounds in the winter? Don't they know about Chick-Fil-A, Wendy's Frosties, Cherry Berry and pizza and hot dogs at Sam's?

Surely The Great and Mighty Papa can get them excused one short day per week. That's it! I have connections. I will pull strings!

No I won't.

It is time.

The boys are clearly ready; "The Great and Mighty" is clearly not. The upside? That one is simple: we have shared a lot of great memories, and there are plenty more memories to be made in the future. Plenty!

>>>--<<<

That is what I will tell myself. This is a good thing. It is better this way. Yes, that is what I will tell myself.

Sometimes you go with whatever helps you sleep...

>>>>> The significance of an individual life is more accurately measured by the compound interest earned upon the ordinary than by the lump sum of the spectacular. <<<<<

Uncovering the Secret

Forgiveness is absolutely essential in any long-term relationship. The fact is, the longer you have been in a relationship, job, or church, the greater the chances that you have been hurt. Not because people are evil or because people intentionally tried to hurt you, but because we live in a fallen world. And in a fallen world, even people of good will who love God and each other will get cross-threaded from time to time.

The key to staying in that relationship, job or church is to forgive. I think there are three keys in play here:

1. **Realize the intent was not to hurt you.** You have to offer the benefit of the doubt here.

2. **Realize that you may be partially to blame in the process.** I have noticed that people who are frustrated at me are people with whom I am frustrated.

3. **Choose to forgive.** That is right. It is a choice, not a disposition.

People who can't renegotiate relationships after being hurt will miss the nearly infinite benefits reaped by both parties in a long-term relationship.

If you have been in your marriage, job, or congregation for a long time, you have a significant investment in that relationship. You have built something significant together. Don't let temporal disappointments rob you of infinitely greater long-term (or even eternal) joys.

What is the secret of successful long term relationships? Forgiveness. Plain and simple.

>>> 10 Things Nobody Needs From Me (or You) <<<

1. My frustration
2. My every opinion
3. My disappointment
4. My pessimism
5. My sarcasm
7. My selfishness
8. My pride
9. My self-righteousness
10. My unforgiveness

Choosing to live a positive life is a win for everyone ... especially for you!

>>>--<<<

Eight Steps to Owning Monday (by Noon)

1. **Clear anything you have been dreading off your desk.** Get all poopy stuff out of the way first.

2. **Return all messages.** All of them.

3. **Attack your "haven't-got-to-it-yet" pile.** Toss what you aren't ever going to get to in the trash.

4. **Congratulate two co-workers or bosses on a recent success.**

5. **Send a note of encouragement to two co-workers or bosses who have really tough jobs.**

6. **Make three direct contacts that could potentially produce something really good in the future.**

7. **Send a thank-you note to a mentor.**

8. **Have a long lunch.** You deserve it!

Congratulations! You have just owned Monday!

>>>--<<<

Why You Can't just Punch Everyone Who 'Boffers' You ...

Over the past years, I have fallen in love with the General Rules of Methodism all over again. I find these three principles readily able to guide me in difficult times: Do no harm. Do all the good you can. Stay in love with God. It is good stuff!

A few of years back, my grandson Maddox was crying when I got home from work. When I asked what was wrong, everyone in the room informed me that he didn't get his way and was being a big baby. I took him to another room and asked if it was true.

"Are you being a big baby because you didn't get your way?"

"Yes."

I responded, "Dude, you are six years old now. You don't use the diaper or drink the bottle. You are a big boy! There will be more and more times as you get older that you don't get your way. A part of being a big boy is to hold it together when you don't get your way and know everything will be okay."

>>>--<<<

And later on that very day, my other grandson Elijah hit his brother Isaac. Just socked him. "Elijah, why did you hit your brother?"

"He was 'boffering' me."

Back to the instruction room.

"Buddy, you are five years old. You don't use the diaper or drink the bottle. You are a big boy! And just because someone is bothering you, doesn't mean you can just punch them. You have to find better ways to work things out."

So here is the bottom line: adult Christians really need to behave better than my preschool-aged grandsons. You can't cry (or make negative posts on social media) every time you don't get your way, and you can't lash out every time someone or something bothers you.

We need to put away childish things. Love demands it.

>>>--<<<

Educated to Succeed
(In a World That no Longer Exists)

Were you formally educated to succeed in a world that no longer exists? I certainly was. Here are my thoughts on these changing times for the church:

History will look upon the years that spanned our lifetimes and declare them to be a period of seismic cultural shift. In the same way the Gutenberg Press changed the world in 1439, the advent of the personal computer has changed the world again. We live in a time when the Norman Rockwell America in which many of us were reared has given away to an emerging world having little in union with the world it replaced. As a result, most of us over fifty were formally educated to succeed in a world that no longer exists.

I graduated from Candler School of Theology at Emory University in 1992 equipped to do ministry in a piano, organ, hymnal, bulletin-led and highly formalized worship world. I came to work each day dressed like a banker or a lawyer. Today I do ministry in a dual-big-screen, four-site, eight-services and two Biker's Churches, rock-and-roll band, internet, social media and unbelievably informal worship world. In the summer I wear shorts to work, for Heaven's sake!

>>>--<<<

We are conducting ministry in a cultural earthquake, where the old world is almost completely gone except for a strong pocket here and there, and the new world is jagged, volatile, and unpredictable. No wonder baby-boomer church leaders have a bit of vocational vertigo. For many, the church has become the last enclave of the old world, where people can still come to exercise power in an economy they understand, worship with familiar forms, slow things down, and take solace in their cultural sanctuary. The problem is that many churches have become "Ecclesiastically Amish," and while they do provide a much-desired and appreciated service to their ever-declining memberships, they are failing miserably their opportunity to continue the ministry of Christ to a new generation.

Our stated mission at Christ Church is that we exist to connect people to Jesus Christ. Every decision we make – from programming, to staffing, to administration, to worship style – has been made in relentless pursuit of this mission. We often make decisions that are not popular and not everything we try works, but we believe the most risky thing you can possibly do in this new world is to act like we are still in the old one.

>>>--<<<

It is clear to me that I can be a bridge (between the old world and the new world) or I can be a dinosaur. I choose to be a bridge.

>>>>> Conserve your emotional energy. Don't just give it away because people demand it.

Don't just give it away because people don't know how to behave civilly. Always save some for the people who really love you. <<<<<

P.S. These are normally the folks you see *after* work.

Living Well

I have this life-bucket called "things I will never regret." I try to put something in it every day.

Breakfasts with my dad go in that bucket. So does making memories with my grandchildren. Spending time in the Bible, date nights with Melissa, traveling and making time for old friends go in as well. Sunday lunches with my mom? In the bucket!

I will never be able to completely fill this bucket, but I want to keep it full enough to be sure there are no regrets when the things I am so often tempted to take for granted are no longer in play.

Live well, dear friends! Keep your hearts open, your spirits soaring and your buckets full!

>>>--<<<

>>>>> People often talk about their difficulty with the parts of the Bible they don't understand.

My problem has never been with that.
The parts of the Bible I don't understand don't bother me very much at all.

My struggle is with the parts of the Bible that I understand perfectly. Those unambiguous, "even a kid could understand them" things that I have such difficulty putting into play.

Loving your difficult neighbor who lives next door is a much tougher gig than the stress of not knowing when Jesus will return.

Believe me. <<<<<

>>>--<<<

I wonder how much enjoyment we miss in our lives simply because we are a bit too tightly wound?

Zambora the Gorilla Woman
(DuQuoin, Illinois, circa 1993)

There is no better grandfather in the world than Fred Bishop. He was born for the job. His instincts are uncanny. No matter what Zec's age, Papa Bishop has been able to maintain an incredible connection with him.

No better illustration could be offered than what happened last summer. We traveled to DuQuoin to attend the State Fair with Mom and Dad. Melissa and Lydia bought wristbands so they could ride rides all night. The rest of us felt that spinning in tight circles, going upside down, and hurtling about might interrupt our intention to eat everything at the fair that was not tied down, still living or was hard enough to break teeth.

After an evening of eating and riding, we were winding down and walking through the midway. Melissa and Lydia were attempting to regain equilibrium and the rest of us were trying not to throw up.

>>>--<<<

Over the other sounds of the fair, I heard a loud-speaker state some pretty miraculous news: Just to our left was the lair of Zambora the Gorilla Woman. The promise was clear; for just one American dollar, you could enter the exhibit and witness the beautiful Zambora transform into a 400-pound gorilla before your very eyes! On the front of the exhibit were paintings of the beautiful (and scantily clad) Zambora, and of a fierce and mighty Gorilla. The line for the spectacle primarily consisted of tattooed people wearing black World Wrestling Federation tee shirts. The excitement was overwhelming them. I watched them enter like sheep, enthusiastically offer their American dollars and disappear from sight. In seconds, an explosion occurred inside the exhibit, the door burst open, smoke poured out and toothless people ran screaming from the gorilla formerly known as Zambora.

After a quick cigarette, Zambora, now changed back into a woman, was out in front again, chained to a cage with a Python wrapped around her neck. The announcer was hard at work scaring up another crowd. Melissa and I looked at the gathering people with pity.

"Who would possibly waste a buck to see that drivel?" I inquired. The second the sentence emerged from my mouth, I saw them, there in the middle of the line: sandwiched in between a heavy-set, braless woman who was smoking a cigarette and three skin-headed juvenile delinquents, stood Dad and Zec. They had their eyes firmly glued upon Zambora, American dollars in hand, and were enjoying the moment like a man who may never have another one. In minutes they were herded with the others inside. Soon, I heard the explosion and Dad and Zec ran from the smoking exhibit.

It was then it occurred to me; Zec has the best grandfather in the world. Every young man should get to go to the fair with someone like Papa Bishop and see Zambora turn into a gorilla all in one night.

>>> 10 Ways to Have a Great Day! <<<

1. Be productive. Move the needle.
2. Focus on improving yourself, not on improving others.
3. Put energy into what you can change, not what you can't.
4. See challenges as opportunities, not threats.
5. Don't spend all your energy at work; save some for home.
6. Pray when you are tempted to worry.
7. Listen for a God "prompting" and follow through on it no matter how small.
8. Encourage everyone around you.
9. Remember there is never a down side to having a great attitude.
10. Rejoice, God gave you another day to live. Make the most of it!

>>>--<<<

Unsubscribe

I am always a bit surprised when people get "fed up" with social media and make a big deal about it. The reality is that we control who we follow, who we befriend and what we post. It is really like complaining about the music on a radio station where you have chosen all the artists.

If someone is consistently offensive to you, then unsubscribe. Afterward, you won't get their stuff anymore. It is that easy!

They will still post all kinds of insensitive and outrageous dumb crap, but you won't get it. Try it, it works great! They just go away.

- Tired of someone's drama? Unsubscribe.
- Too many nasty political posts? Unsubscribe.
- Tired of habitually bad attitudes? Unsubscribe.
- Always get upset when *that* person posts? Unsubscribe.

This post has so inspired me that I have critically looked at all my recent Tweets and posts.

I think I will unsubscribe from myself.

>>>--<<<

Overwhelmed? It probably isn't as bad as you think!

When the "Mice" are Just a Mouse

A couple of years back, we heard what sounded like a *mischief* (I Googled it: this is the correct word for lots of mice) of rodents in our ceiling. We were mortified. How do what must have been three hundred mice get in your attic, all at once? I ran to Lowe's and bought seventy-five pounds of poison and various and sundry traps and set them everywhere. Then we braced for the mouse holocaust.

The next morning, only one trap had been successful and it contained one smallish mouse. As I geared up to catch the other two-hundred and ninety-nine, I noted something throughout the day. The noises were gone. Where could the others be? Then it occurred to me: there was only one mouse all along!

I wonder how many times in our lives do we get overwhelmed by what turns out to be a "one-mouse" problem? If you are on a rough patch of highway today, remember things are seldom as bad as they appear ... It is often not a mischief at all, but just one really noisy mouse!

Turn a Bad Day Into a Horrible Day

Having a bad day? Don't waste it! In fact, make it horrible. Here's how it works: The second you know that a day is swirling down the proverbial toilet (with no hope for improvement), immediately tie into it every single thing you have been avoiding for the past several weeks, and do it all that very day. Seriously!

- That phone call you have been avoiding: make it!
- That conversation you have been avoiding: have it!
- That situation you have been avoiding: wade right in!

That's right! Make it the worst day ever!

The cool thing is that when you arrive at work tomorrow, all those things you have been avoiding forever have been done. And that will make tomorrow a great day … perhaps even fabulous!

Never, never, never waste a perfectly bad day! Turn it into a horrible day!

Your tomorrow is looking better already …

Life Hacks Collection No. 2

- Expect attack after times of great spiritual celebration. Satan always wants the ground back he just lost.
- Christianity is a personal relationship with God through Jesus .. with all of its messiness; it is seldom organized and is never a religion.
- These days, I am more concerned about staying in relationship than with always being right. This does not mean I don't want to be right ...
- The long-term effect of sin in an individual life is complexity. The more sin, the more drama.
- Don't focus on driving out the darkness; focus on getting more light inside ... the light will drive away the darkness.
- I have never had a single person tell me their life was better since they quit going to church.
- Take one giant step forward on your faith journey today ... then hold your ground. Repeat tomorrow.
- If you don't think God has specific opinions on things, you have never read Leviticus.

How I (Don't) Want to Live

I have been thinking a lot about how I want to live. Actually, I have been thinking more about how I *don't* want to live.

First of all, I don't want to live with unforgiveness in my heart. I could; in fact, I think it's much easier than forgiving, but I just don't want to.

Second, I don't want to live angry. There are plenty of things to get mad about, and some of those things honestly should make us mad, but I don't want to live that way. I have never found that love and anger share the same space very well.

Third, I don't want to live cautiously. It's not that I am reckless, it's just that I want to live a life that "plays to *win*" and not one that "plays *not to lose*." I want to live fully, and if I make an impact for the better in the tiny space I occupy on this spinning ball, so much the better.

It occurs to me that in answering these three big questions about how I don't want to live, that I have determined just how I wish to live. To choose forgiveness means the hard work of actually forgiving those who have hurt me is on the table.

To choose love requires me to control my impulses, speak and write thoughtfully and to live in future hope, even and especially when, the present is biting solid wood.

To live fully requires letting go of things like security and comfort that conspire to make me live a lesser life.

As we ponder the quality of our lives, we do well to remember that Jesus came to give us precisely the lives we could have never lived without him.

"I have come that they might have life, and have life abundantly." (John 10:10)

Choose life!

>>>--<<<

You will never move forward by staring behind you.

Admit your mistakes.
Ask God to forgive you.
Ask those you have hurt to forgive you.
Ask for forgiveness where you have hurt others.
Make things right where you can.
Turn your attention forward.
Forgive yourself.
Get your head up.
Many adventures lie ahead!

Your story isn't even close to being over ...

Often when you create a memory for someone else, you create a memory for yourself, too.

Andy the Janitor
(Fairview Heights, Illinois, circa 2000)

"Remember" is one of my favorite English words. It is a much more potent and powerful word than its diminutive synonyms like "recall" or "recollect."

For me, remember is best thought of as the antonym of "dismember." To dismember is to tear apart; to remember – or re-member – is to put back together.

I often tell my congregation that though most of us can shower, dress up, put on some cologne and look normal for an hour and a half each Sunday, the reality is that many of the people sitting in our pews are dismembered. We are haunted by past abuses and mistakes, torn by broken promises and failed relationships, and ravaged by disappointment and physical disease. We are hurt, lonely, and afraid, and we come before a holy God in hopes of healing, friendship and hope. I think one of the most Christian things we can do is to remember people.

>>>--<<<

Andy Leahy was the custodian at Christ Church during my first few years here. He had white hair, a closely trimmed beard and piercing blue eyes; he was about five foot ten and couldn't have weighed 140 pounds. By the time I came along, he was a very old man with poor eyesight and limited energy, but Andy had a quality I really admire in a person; he liked me. And I liked him. As the church grew in the very early 2000s, his workload became overwhelming and he retired to care for his ailing wife before finally moving to the East Coast with his children.

On occasion, Andy and I would go out for lunch. He liked to go for fried fish at a historic bar called the Dandy Inn. He always ordered a beer and I ordered a Coke (this was in my pre-Diet Coke days). He reminded me each time we went to lunch that the beer was okay; he was a Lutheran.

I would eat and Andy would sip his beer and talk. Andy told me about World War II, his life as a Seabee, the things he had done, the pain he had encountered and the places he had been. He said he dared not speak of such things at home; by my reckoning, he had about sixty years of conversation and recollections pent up inside him.

As he spoke, he would sometimes be overcome by emotion and stop talking, eat for a moment with a

>>>--<<<

shaking right hand, wipe the tears from his eyes, take a drink and then resume.

On our final lunch before Andy retired, I noted two rough-hewn men sitting in the next booth were listening to every word Andy said as he spoke at length about his service in the Pacific during World War II. We were getting ready to leave when one of the men got out of his seat and literally blocked Andy's path to the door. I was frankly unsure of his intentions and stood at full alert.

He said, "Sir, I couldn't help but overhear what you were saying. I just wanted to shake your hand and say thank you for what you did for us over there."

Andy was literally dazed. It was clear he was in new territory. As if called to attention, Andy stood up straight and tall and extended a trembling hand. Tears began to roll down both of our cheeks as he grasped the stranger's hand and looked him dead in the eye. Andy the Janitor had just been remembered.

It was the last time I ever saw Andy.

Life Hacks Collection No. 3

- The witness of an authentic and stubborn faith that holds in the hurricane is the best testimony we have to offer this world.
- My problem is not that I don't love some people; it is that I don't live close enough to God to let Him love them through me ...
- The "sin that so easily besets you" needs to be drowned in baptismal water every day.
- Every sinful and hurtful thing begins with a single impulse not brought under the submission of Christ.
- When we are living the Spirit-filled life, God will sometimes lead us into situations out of which only God can deliver us!
- The big idea of Christianity is never to try harder; it is an invitation to be transformed entirely.
- Sometimes Jesus loves on me and sometimes Jesus shoves on me. What He never does is conform to what I think He ought to be.
- Jesus is always asking of us what we least want to give Him.

Tiny Flames of Hope (and the Rod Stewart Channel)

Today, I was troubled. I went outside by myself, lit a little fire in our fire pit in broad daylight, and thought about the state of the world. I put Pandora on my Rod Stewart channel and they played the Eagles, Sting, and Fleetwood Mac. I heard one, count it, just one Rod Stewart song. You will have that …

I soon found that not even music could soothe me, and frankly the exercise seemed depressing and overwhelming. I began to hope the fire would go out so I could just go in. There is so much pain, division, suspicion and flat out horror surrounding us and not just today but every day.

Looking into that little fire calmed my spirits: The dancing flames, the crack of the wood, the smell of smoke. Then it hit me: you and I can't eradicate the darkness in this world, but we can light fires of hope and compassion ... to give light and offer warmth. Seemingly small ones though they be.

So let's just keep on tending the flames of hope and keep on praying, loving and believing. Knowing that as the day inevitability turns to night, our little fires will shine more brightly than ever.

I read a lot of stuff about "Christians." When I finish such articles and blogs, I often think, "I am not that *kind of Christian. Which brings a question to mind ...*

What Kind of Christian am I?

1. I am the kind of Christian whose faith has not rendered me angry, uptight, paranoid or humorless.

2. I am the kind of Christian who chooses to be known by what I am for, much more so than by what I am against.

3. I am the kind of Christian who does not believe I am any better than anyone else.

4. I am the kind of Christian who honestly believes that Christ is the answer to the questions of forgiveness, purpose and community.

5. I am the kind of Christian who believes I am saved because God is good all the time and not because I am good some of the time.

6. I am the kind of Christian who is much more offended by the sin in me than by the sin in others.

>>>--<<<

7. I am the kind of Christian who believes the Gospel is actually really, really Good News.

8. I am the kind of Christian who believes Jesus is the way, the truth and the life.

9. I am the kind of Christian who does not believe the sins I am least dispositioned to commit are the worst sins of all.

10. I am the kind of Christian who seeks to be an objective, empathetic person of conscience and is not too proud to admit that I find it most difficult at times.

11. I am the kind of Christian who believes unconditional love does not require unconditional approval.

12. I am the kind of Christian who places greater hope in God's grip on me than my grip on God.

13. I am the kind of Christian who is flawed, imperfect, fallen and ... forgiven.

What kind of Christian are you? You will have to answer that one for yourself ...

>>>--<<<

Why Christians Don't *Have* to go to Church

The question never quite goes away, "Do Christians *have* to go to church?"

Here are my thoughts:

It seems to me that Christianity is a vertical relationship with God that is lived horizontally within the life of the local church. The church is the team, Christians are the players. Nothing makes less theological sense to me than the thought that there is little or no linkage between Christ and His Church. The New Testament establishes that the Church *is* the physical presence of Christ until Christ returns. It is the only game in town. Period.

Do you know what you call a baseball player without a team? A bat owner. Baseball is a team sport and there is no concept of an individual player apart from a team. Baseball is about the team, not the player. A Christian who sees no need for the church is like a baseball player who sees no need for a team. A skilled player not on a team is a loss at best and a waste at worst.

I am sometimes asked, "Do you *have* to go to church to be a true Christian?" My response is,

"Absolutely not! True Christians will *want* to go to church."

>>>>> The Road to Emmaus story reminds us the lost are not always thieves on crosses; they are sometimes disciples walking the wrong direction. The other thing to keep in mind is that at the very time they were walking away from Jesus, Jesus was walking toward them. <<<<<

>>>--<<<

Staying With the Herd

When I was a kid I loved to watch Mutual of Omaha's *Wild Kingdom,* which ran from 1963 to 1985. I literally grew up with the show. It starred St. Louis zookeeper Marlin Perkins. Back then, "wild" animal shows were more "tame" than they are today and a lot more was left to the imagination.

It always seemed to me the show was disproportionately set in Africa and lions were rock stars. Wildebeests were kind of like bit actors on the old *Star Trek* series; if they managed to get on the transporter at all, they were unlikely to return to the ship. Here was the scene that plays in my mind; a pride of near-starving lionesses approaches a massive herd of migrating wildebeests (the male lions were normally posing, roaring, preening and resting ... mainly resting). As the herd becomes collectively aware of the lions, it shifts and packs in tightly.

Then you see it all unfold from the helicopter: one of the young, sick, or old gets separated from the herd. At this point I am screaming at my black-and-white television set (with tinfoil-wrapped rabbit ears), "Go back to the herd! Go back!" (I always did root for the underdogs: or in this case, the *underbeests*). Then you see the pride loop around, offer quick chase, attack the flanks and then one goes for the jugular. At this point they cut away to commercial and the gory details were left to your imagination while they tried to sell you life insurance.

Getting too far from the herd is a dangerous enterprise for wildebeests in the Serengeti. So is getting too far from the church in a fallen world.

Prayer for a Troubled World

Almighty God, in the midst of a troubled world, use me as an instrument of healing and hope.

Be with the sick, comfort the mourning, mend the broken-hearted and calm troubled minds. Give me the grace to believe the best about others, the eyes to see your guiding hand in all circumstances and a heart that refuses to surrender hope.

As I love you and love my neighbor this week, make me quick to listen, slow to speak, and grant me an abiding and contagious respect for all of your Creation.

In the strong Name of Jesus, Amen!

The Upside of a Bad Relationship with God

I have been thinking about what it means to have a relationship with God.

First of all, to be in relationship means you know something of another. You may not know everything, and some of what you think you know may well be wrong, but you know something of each other.

Secondly, it does not necessarily imply that the relationship is good. We all have relationships that are a bit rocky or have traversed some rough patches of highway. Even the best of relationships get cross-threaded now and then. Some people are cross-threaded with God.

Good relationship? No. Relationship? Yes.

Since the Bible teaches that relationship comes at the initiative of God, anyone who is struggling with God is doing so because God is reaching out to them. People with no relationship with God don't struggle with God at all. In fact they seldom think of God, and if they do it is dispassionately; like a discussion about a baseball game that really doesn't interest them, or about the weather in the fall. If you are thinking about God, be assured God is thinking about you.

Sometimes we get concerned because we – or people we know – are struggling with their faith. They don't have it all figured out and we wish they did. They are angry with God and we wish they weren't. I would remind you that the very act of struggle is clear evidence of relationship. No one struggles with strangers or those they care nothing about.

If you are struggling with God, take heart. Keep knocking, yelling, asking, weeping and seeking. God can handle your pain, your questions, your issues, your doubt and even your bad theology. It is only when the gloves come off, the gauntlet is thrown and raw honesty sets in that we can face our issues. Ugly? Perhaps. Necessary? Absolutely!

Stay in the struggle. Keep attending church when you don't feel like going. Keep worshiping when you don't feel like singing. Keep believing when you don't understand, and stay at the table when what you want to do is run away.

And one day you will find, much to your surprise, you have made it through the storm and that you were loved every step of the way ...

The upside of a bad relationship? It is still a relationship. And that is something you can build upon.

>>>>> It is a whole lot easier to demonize folks who may sin differently than we do than it is to deal with the sin in our own lives. <<<<<

Life Hacks Collection No. 4

- I believe God will forgive you every time you fall, but I equally believe God appreciates not having to do it every five minutes.
- Sin will put you in one cage and legalism will put you in another, but a cage is a cage. Jesus came to set us free.
- Faith in a fallen world is like running up a down going escalator … the second you stop moving forward, you are headed the wrong direction.
- Personal holiness is Spirit-empowered self-management.
- Spiritual ground is not hard to take; it is hard to retain.
- Prayer in desperate times forces us beyond the rhetoric of our faith.
- God is not interested in the shortest distance between two points; God is interested in the relationship along the way.
- God is not a D.J.; prayer is not a request line.
- We are a bit peculiar with justice and grace.
- Justice is what we want for others. Grace is what we want for ourselves.

Jesus is Not Your Lovely Spokesmodel

Too many people today want to put words into the mouth of Jesus. They attempt to create Jesus in their own image and then immediately sign him to endorse their products, promote their politics and galvanize their social positions. That is something we just can't do. It must not be allowed.

Jesus spoke for God and His Kingdom, not for us. He clearly stated his mission (to seek and to save the lost), taught about his Kingdom and made clear his core values. He was fearless, counter-cultural, counter-intuitive and absolutely not for sale!

They did not crucify Jesus because he was always holding cute lambs, posing for paintings and being compliant; they did so because he wrecked their sensibilities, crushed their pride and exposed their hypocrisy. The same way he wrecks our sensibilities, crushes our pride and exposes our hypocrisy.

The Pharisees, Sadducees, King Herod and the Romans could not buy off, "handle," co-opt or silence Jesus, nor can we. Jesus is who he is. Not who we want him to be.

We must either embrace the Jesus of the Bible or reject him outright. But we don't get to hijack him.

Four Deal-Breaking Faith Convictions

1. Jesus is the way, the truth and the life. No one comes to the Father but by him.

2. The person of Jesus is the most reliable testament to God, and the Bible is the most reliable testament to Jesus.

3. Love must be the defining characteristic of the Christian community.

4. We don't all have to agree on everything to go to church together, but we do have to agree on items 1-3.

The Downside of Forgiveness (Doesn't Exist)

I have been thinking about forgiveness tonight. Not micro-forgiveness, but forgiveness of the macro variety.

There is a popular misconception that forgiveness is an altruistic notion; a lofty plane only the saintly can hope to obtain. I disagree. Forgiveness is really more pragmatic than you may imagine. There is a lot in it for us when we choose to forgive!

Here are my thoughts:

1. We don't forgive to let those who have mistreated us off the hook; we forgive to let ourselves off the hook of bitterness and hate.

2. When we forgive, we break the power those who have hurt us have over us. They no longer control our thoughts and emotions.

3. Forgiveness of others places us in position to be forgiven by God.

4. Forgiving someone does not exonerate them from God's judgment.

5. Forgiveness returns the power that was stolen from us, by putting us in a proactive, not a reactive position in our lives.

When we forgive, we release ourselves from emotional bondage, break the power of our oppressors, place ourselves in right standing with God, turn those who have harmed us over to God's judgment and enable ourselves to regain control of ourselves and our situation.

Downside? Not seeing one.

Could it be that Jesus was right about this forgiveness stuff all along?

>>>--<<<

Bible Readings From the Deer Stand

I led a group of some 200 people who read the Bible from cover to cover in 2015.

We had been in Isaiah for a long while, and I must confess to being more than a bit bogged down. For days I read out of pure discipline (me being the leader and all) but it was not easy sledding. And then one incredible day ... the Word burst open before me and God spoke directly to my heart concerning some very specific leadership issues. What a day!

It reminds me a bit of deer hunting: you go out and put the cold hours in day after day and see nothing. Nothing. You are cold and miserable. Miserable and cold.

And then one day … that big buck walks up to your tree, and BOOM! What a day!

Faithfulness in the Christian disciplines is not always easy; in fact, sometimes it's just plain hard. You read and get nothing and pray and hear nothing. But still you read. And still you pray.

And then one incredible day ... BOOM!

Stay in the hunt my friends ... your day will come!

Life Hacks Collection No. 5

- God will never reveal Himself to us in ways that negate the need for faith!
- "Lead us not into temptation" is a prayer best prayed with the assistance of clear personal and professional boundaries.
- I think the hole in most of our lives is the gap between good intention and meaningful action.
- Materialism is a religion of accumulation and all it can promise is more of what it has failed to deliver in the first place.
- I have no patience these days for critics who have accomplished nothing and have strong opinions on everything. None at all.
- I have given up cynicism. It is just too easy ...
- Once you know a person's character and core values, their actions get highly predictable.
- Praying "thy Kingdom come, thy will be done on Earth as it is in Heaven," is a prayer of spiritual warfare.
- True temptation is often not toward evil; it is the enticement to embrace a lesser destiny.

Does Unconditional Love Necessitate Unconditional Approval?

I strive to treat everyone really well.
People who agree with me and people who disagree with me. People who treat me well and people who treat me poorly. I am going to treat people well. Already decided.

But I will also not be bullied into condoning sin, in myself or in others. It is actually my absolute conviction that I am a sinner that compels me to treat other sinners (though they may sin differently than me) really well. People who forget they are sinners get filled with pride and do great harm. They get thinking they are "all that and a bag of communion wafers." I don't want to do harm, ever.

Some clearly think unconditional love requires absolute approval concerning the decisions, lifestyle choices and actions of the beloved. I disagree. Others feel that absolute rejection of the individual must accompany any disapproval of behavior. I again disagree. When one's Christianity encourages them to behave in graceless ways, there is clearly a glitch in their operating system.

In my construct, unconditional love does not require unconditional acceptance, but it does require civility, respect and grace.

>>>--<<<

I will never be a bully. I don't want to associate with bullies. On the other hand, I am not going to be bullied, either. My views are going to be based upon my interpretation of Scripture. When the sensibilities of this culture are long forgotten, the Bible will still be shining like a new dime!

Game. Set. Match.

God loves you.
Just the way you are.
Despite what you have done.
God is crazy about you.
And there is nothing, good or bad, you can do to change this simple fact.

For many, this is a difficult concept because you have never been loved well.
You have been loved poorly; or more accurately, conditionally: You were accepted when you performed to standard.
You were rejected when you did not.

God is not like that.
God just loves.
It is all He knows how to do.

What Chick-Fil-A Understands

I am sitting in Chick-Fil-A. I just had a meeting and am catching up on messages before I head into work. There is instrumental Christian music playing (though I am unsure how instrumental music can be Christian), and I am thinking about this company. Brandon, the franchise owner, just stopped by and shook my hand. Asked how softball is going. Personal touch. Appreciated. The restaurant is clean, the people are nice and the food is good.

This is a Christian operation. No doubt about it. They are closed on Sundays. Their corporation has made clear stands for families and traditional values. They have taken plenty of heat, but they just keep smiling, saying "my pleasure," catering to families and serving chicken sandwiches.

It occurs to me that Chick-fil-A is unapologetically Christian but they aren't in a bad mood about it. In fact, they seem absolutely delighted.

That is precisely what we need in our world today: Unapologetic Christians who are not in a bad mood about it!

>>>--<<<

>>>>> Positive thinking is a wonderful thing. Just don't confuse it with the Gospel. <<<<<

Don't Confuse Maturity With Stagnation

I increasingly wonder if we don't often mistake spiritual stagnation for Christian maturity. I am thinking we need to measure Christian growth less in terms of duration and more in terms of intensity. Perhaps, "I have been a Christian for thirty years" carries far less weight than, "I am head over heels in love with Jesus and growing in my faith."

I have noticed over the years that successful people, regardless of what they do, are constantly striving to get smarter, better and more effective. They are never content, and have an inner hunger to learn and grow. Conversely, less-successful people often think they already know everything. They are the first to declare themselves "experts," not realizing the cutting edge of their field is now light years ahead of them.

It is the same with our spiritual lives. A lot of people categorize Christians on a linear spectrum that has "mature" on one end and "Immature" on the other but I think this is dangerous. Not to the immature folks, they are just fine, but for the folks who have determined they are mature.

Just what exactly does mature mean? Does it mean you have arrived? Does it mean you have it all, you've got it down and school is out forever?

I don't want to sound harsh but some of the most prideful, mean-spirited, divisive, judgmental and un-Christ-like people I have ever met would have been the first to tell you they were mature Christians.

Is it possible that how far along the Christian journey you think you are, is not nearly as important as which direction you are headed?

Perhaps we need to rethink how we think about Christian growth altogether. These days, I tend to categorize the spectrum with "growing" on one end and "stagnated" on the other:

Characteristics of Growing Christians:

1. Passionate about Jesus: They have palpable excitement!
2. Launching into deeper water: They are engaged in things to stretch them, shove on them and make them better.
3. Constantly giving jesus more: They learn more, give more, serve more, stretch more and live more.
4. Humility: They compare themselves only with God.
5. Teachable spirit: They know they need to continue to learn.
6. Great attitudes: They have a "can-do" spirit.

Characteristics of Stagnated Christians:

1. Lack of passion for Jesus: Whatever it is that excites them these days, it isn't Jesus.
2. Frozen discipleship: Their level of commitment, giving, service, involvement or discipleship (though perhaps significant) hasn't increased in years.
3. Lack of increased effort: They are doing what they have always done, reading what they have always read, praying what they have always prayed; coasting and mailing it in.
4. Prideful: They compare themselves with others.

5. Critical spirit: They think they know it all.
6. Negative attitudes: They have a "can't-do spirit"

Seriously ponder these things. Do you display more characteristics of the first or the second list? Are you growing or are you stagnant?

I believe a new Christian growing is in far better position with God than a lifelong Christian who is stagnated.

>>>--<<<

Holidays

I never quite know what to do with Christmas materials so I grouped it together. Here is Christmas, with all its tinsel, high wattage and complexity.

The Holiday Hangover

Life does not always go the way you figured it would. It bounces far more like a football than a basketball. It is wildly unpredictable.

I am discovering that a key to happiness is learning to appreciate what you have more than you lament what you have lost. This is admittedly a discipline, because I don't think human nature takes us there on our own. I believe that in a fallen world, we are inclined to be miserable, not happy. Happiness is something for which we have to work, and work hard.

Back in time is the one place none of us can ever go; it is sobering but true. So we must press forever forward, with a very real hope that joy and happiness lie ahead for us.

We must keep on doing the right things for the right reasons, trusting we will get the right results in the right time.

God has a future and a hope for you! Believe it!

Keep the faith dear friends ... keep the faith.

>>>--<<<

>>>>> Everybody wants that "burning bush" encounter with God. They demand it. They want to know for sure, see something extraordinary, and hear the voice of God with their own ears. In the history of the world it happened once.

It's probably not going to happen for you. <<<<<

>>>--<<<

A Room in the Inn
(Fairview Heights, Illinois, circa 1997)

It was late December 1997, and we were about to celebrate our first Christmas in Fairview Heights. We had run down to DuQuoin Friday and Saturday for a holiday gift exchange with my mom and dad, and were on our way back.

When we arrived at the parsonage late Saturday night, it was clear that something was wrong at our home on Keelan Drive. I left the family in the car and cautiously unlocked the front door of the house. As I slowly opened the door, a cold wind bit my face. The frigid draft that assaulted me was from the back sliding glass door, which had been forcibly opened. It stood wide open, with the drapes dancing to the beat of a harsh winter wind.

The parsonage had been ransacked. The burglars had invaded our space, gone through our drawers and cabinets, took what they wanted – and worst of all, they'd stolen our Christmas gifts. I called the police and a couple of church leaders.

The House of Bishop was shaken to the core. Would this event define our entire Fairview Heights ministry? Would fear enter my children and family? I felt lost in a strange and far-away place.

>>>--<<<

As we worked with the police, a couple from the church came by and extended an invitation to let us stay the night with them. We jumped at the offer. It appears there was room in the inn after all.

I suppose we learned something that night of Christmas. It was all about a young family with nowhere to stay and about the grace in finding a much-needed room for the night. It was about Christian love and compassion lived out in a way that brings warmth in a cold world.

The next week, Christmas gifts for the kids began to pour in from the congregation; by the time Christmas came around, we were no longer in an unfamiliar place surrounded by strangers; instead, we were in our new home surrounded by family.

This Christmas, I will tell my grandchildren this story, right after I read the Christmas story from the Bible and just before they open their presents. It will teach them that Christmas didn't just happen in Bethlehem some two thousand years ago ... it is still happening today in the places where our feet touch the ground!

For me, the wonder of Christmas has always been most evident in a childhood memory – and a pitcher of Teem.

A Story About Jesus Turning Water Into Teem (*Somewhere in Arkansas, circa 1975*)

Growing up the child of a missionary-evangelist involved its share of uncertainty, but one thing remained constant throughout the years of my childhood: we came home for Christmas. There were years that we couldn't afford many gifts, but we always arrived in Sunfield, Illinois, for the Christmas Eve program at the Methodist Church. After the program, Santa would come out, and I always wondered how he knew I was going to be there (being that we were from out of state and all), but each year I received a gift.

One Christmas we were just barely able to afford the pilgrimage from Texas to Illinois. We stopped for lunch along the interstate, at a restaurant called Tastee World, a companion to a Days Inn motel. We went in, and as we intently gazed at the menu, Dad broke the news to us that we could not afford soft drinks. When Dad ordered a pitcher of water instead, my face must have shown the horror of hearing those terrible words, but we had long since learned to make the best of things.

>>>--<<<

When the waitress returned, she said in a most chipper voice, "Here is your water," and poured it into our empty glasses. I picked up my glass, took a drink, and my taste buds began to soar: powerfully, wonderfully, infinitely; it was TEEM! Teem, the lemon-lime soft drink, complete with delicious bubbles and wondrous bouquet. A little later the waitress asked if we needed more water and returned with another pitcher of Teem. She winked at me with a compassionate smirk that revealed we had a little secret.

I don't remember what Santa gave me that year at Sunfield Methodist, or what my parents got for me, for that matter, but I do remember the most wonderful gift ever received: a pitcher of Teem at a Tastee World restaurant, from a waitress I didn't know in a town I don't remember.

Perhaps baby Jesus on that special day turned the water into Teem just for a little boy going home for Christmas.

Dealing With Disappointment
(During the Holidays)

It is 100-percent certain that during this holiday season, you will be dealing with people who have disappointed you.

When we are around people who have disappointed us in one way or the other, a myriad of emotions are sent into frenzy by our brain; particularly if these people who have hurt us are people we also love. We see that person and the emotional dam breaks loose, and we are suddenly flooded by a cacophony of thoughts and feelings.

We have no control over these impulses. What we can control is what we do with them.
For me, there are only three options for dealing with unavoidable people who have disappointed you (or who continue to disappoint you).

1. **We can declare them pariahs, do our very best to avoid them. and treat them rudely.** This is clearly an option, and in some cases (like when there has been abuse), it may be the right option – but not usually.

2. **We can be polite to them but choose not to engage beyond that point.** This is really not a bad strategy if you are really hurting, but it is a

temporary one. This strategy is best used in the immediate aftermath of disappointment, when we have not yet sorted out our own feelings, much less determined how we will engage or not engage the person who has hurt us.

3. **We can forgive them and choose to renegotiate the relationship.** Forgiveness does not let the person who hurt you off the hook; rather, it lets you off the hook of being vengeful and bitter toward them. On the other hand, we can't simply act like nothing ever happened. It did. A conversation to negotiate the relationship on the other side of disappointment is necessary, but don't have that conversation until you are truly ready. The right conversation held before you are emotionally ready to have it is always the wrong conversation.

Forgiveness is not an easy option, but it is the only Christian one. And if you are wondering how you can forgive those who have sinned against you, keep in mind that God has forgiven your sins against Him. You don't have to get things completely figured out this season, but a determination to get things headed in the right direction is a win no matter how you slice it.

Life does not always unfold the way that we plan or hope. We have no control over this. What we do have control over is our attitudes and our actions. The key is to take what we have before us and make the very best of it and that is always a choice.

Choose forgiveness. Choose love. Choose life.

>>>>> Mary and Joseph remind us that God reserves the right to alter the trajectory of the lives of ordinary people. People like you and me. <<<<<

>>>--<<<

Life in the Fish Bowl

We often think that our most powerful witness comes from a position of strength. How we glory in what little we get right! In reality, our most powerful witness comes from a position of weakness.

>>>--<<<

Being a Papa is one of the few things in my life that didn't turn out to be overrated.

Crazy About Them (Poop-a-Geddon)
(Fairview Heights, Illinois, circa 2013)

Fridays are normally a day with the grandchildren. Melissa watches all four of them each weekday, and since I take Fridays off, we are all in the house together all day. I used to sleep in every Friday, take the dog on a late walk, take a shower, eat some lunch out and then piddle for the rest of the day, but that was before we had grandchildren. Things are different now.

Last Friday, I had planned to take my oldest grandson, Maddox, to Chick-Fil-A. This one-on-one time always goes well and it gives Melissa a three-to-one ratio with the little ones for a couple of hours. However, I discovered that my grandson Elijah was coming along, and suddenly it didn't seem right to leave granddaughter Mabry at home. In a moment of extreme courage, I determined to take all three of them (ages four, three and two) to Chick-Fil-A, alone.

I loaded up Melissa's Jeep Commander, installed car seats (two of which are the size of living room recliners), and secured the tribe. I left one-year-old Isaac with Melissa and was feeling pretty good

>>>--<<<

about myself. I was clearly demonstrating servant leadership (this being my day off and all) by taking three children off of Melissa's hands for a couple of hours and opening the door for some bonding time and for great memories with Papa. In a moment of temporary sanity, I called my dad to see if he wanted to come along, but when he heard I had all three of the kids, he made up a lame excuse as to why he was not coming. I was on my own.

When I arrived, I set them each free of their car restraints and we all held hands while crossing the parking lot. Things were going so well, until I opened the door. I don't know what possessed Elijah, but he immediately ran to the condiment section and began throwing packets of mayonnaise across the serving area. I quickly reprimanded him, then went to place our orders.

Once seated, just across from the glass-enclosed play area, I fixed their drinks and prepared their meals. Then Mabry saw Elijah's chocolate milk and suddenly forgot that she had told me two minutes earlier that she wanted lemonade. The second I got her calmed down, I noted that Elijah was crushing his round hash browns in his hand, and had already thrown several under the table at Maddox.

>>>--<<<

I had forgotten napkins, so I scooted to the front – leaving the kids – and grabbed a handful to use to clean up the tater tots, when I noticed all three children were standing on their seats looking over the divider at me, yelling "Poop!" You have to understand, poop is the worst word they know and they always get in trouble for saying poop but now all three were yelling "Poop!" and laughing uncontrollably.

Once we had survived lunch (and the "poop-a-geddon"); it was time for the easy part: turning them loose in the glass-enclosed, soundproof and perfectly safe play land. I ushered them inside and reached into my pocket for my phone to check messages and have some "Shane time."

"Poop, I left my phone in the car," I thought to myself. Running for napkins seemed acceptable, but actually leaving the building seemed irresponsible. I thought about asking one of the exceptionally polite restaurant workers to run and get my phone, and I assume they would have responded, "My pleasure," but that, too, seemed a stretch. I was going to have to go without a phone.

Then I heard something from the soundproof room: they were screaming – not because they were hurt or mad – they were just screaming to see how loud they could scream. At this point, I imagined that they were someone else's grandchildren (this technique had worked great with my kids), but when I looked up, Maddox and Elijah had climbed on top of the interior door handle and were jumping off, and Mabry had somehow managed to abscond with Elijah's chocolate milk, take it into the play area where she spilled it all over the floor.

It was at this point that I considered locking the play area, calling both sets of parents, informing them their children were locked inside, and leaving. Instead, I went back for more napkins and cleaned up the mess.

Now at my wit's end, I told them we were leaving because they could not obey. They all three ran into the tubular slide, where I could hear them laughing and saying "Poop!" Finally, I coaxed them out, put on their shoes, and got them headed towards the door where we exited. We held hands across the parking-lot-of-shame and reloaded into their seats. I started the car and swore we were never going to do this again, and then I looked in the rearview mirror.

They were absolutely ... beautiful. Those little disobedient, "poop"-slinging snot-wads were absolutely beautiful.

>>>--<<<

They are my descendants, my legacy, my people and my tribe. I am absolutely crazy about them! Not because they are always good (that day, they were *not* good), but because they are always mine.

I think God sees us the same way. We are His creation, His reflection, His people and His tribe.

He is crazy about us!

Not because we are good, but because we are His!

>>>--<<<

Sometimes being a pastor is fun. Possibly too fun.

**Praying on the Spot
(The Miracle in the Frozen Food Aisle)**
(Sumner, Illinois, circa 1994)

In my five years as pastor of the Sumner/Beulah Charge, I seldom had time to visit our shut-ins with any regularity. Sumner ran about 250 a Sunday and Beulah ran about 150; either congregation should have been a full-time job. When you factored in that the nearest real hospital was an hour-and-a-half away, there was seldom time to do anything but sermon preparation, attend church meetings and visit shut-ins.

It really wasn't as bad as you might think on the shut-in front, because I often ran into them at Wal-Mart, the restaurant at Red Hill State Park or the Key Market Grocery Store.

One day our family was at the Key Market and I saw one of our Sumner shut-ins in the canned goods aisle. She had spotted me first and was hoping to avoid me by looping around the frozen food section and making a getaway while I was in the back of the store. This was unbelievably ambitious for an 88-year-old woman with limited mobility in a 1,800-square-foot grocery store, but she gave it a try. I respected her for it.

>>>--<<<

Sensing her dubious intentions (and feeling like this could be fun), I sprinted to the front of the store, looped around, and when she arrived at the frozen foods aisle, I was standing face-to-face with her.

I smiled and asked, "How are you doing today?" She was now in an old-fashioned conundrum. I could see it on her face. She had stated on many occasions that she was too ill to attend church, but here she was standing under her own power (and moving with surprising speed) in the old Key Market. I couldn't wait for her response!

She looked down, gathered her wits, took a long breath, then started outlining her maladies for me, from the top of her psoriasis-afflicted scalp to the bottom of her corn-infested feet.

When she had talked herself out, I said, "Sister, may I pray for you?" Normally, I would have said, "I'll be praying for you," but not today. We were well beyond that ... too much was invested in this encounter.

She responded, "Right here in the frozen food aisle?"

I said, "Yes ma'am," and didn't wait for an invitation. I did not use the "inside voice" mom

>>>--<<<

had taught me as a kid, as I launched into a ten-minute, high-volume prayer in which I asked God to heal each of her various illnesses and discomforts by name. I prayed that her mysterious "Sunday sickness" that prohibited her from worshipping with God's people but allowed her to shop in grocery stores would be healed, and summarily offered various and sundry other petitions for her as I felt led.

When I finished, a smiling crowd had gathered and she was moving toward the door so quickly that she almost forgot to pay. I checked out, got in my car and thought, "Love it!"

Want to hear the rest of the story? Here it comes! Often we have no idea if or how God answered the prayers we offer for people, but this story is an exception. It appears that in the after-math of our holy encounter in the frozen food aisle, a miracle occurred!

A few weeks later I ran into the same shut-in at the Wal-Mart in Lawrenceville; I caught her eye and yelled across the store, "Great to see you, sister! How are you feeling today?"

She replied with a resounding, "FANTASTIC!" with more energy and life than I had ever

>>>--<<<

encountered from her. She nearly did a dance to prove it!

She was healed! The Lord certainly works in mysterious ways.

Yes sir ... I have been praying on the spot ever since!

>>>--<<<

What is Wrong with 'Shane Shane?'
(Fairview Heights, Illinois, circa 2012)

When God created humanity, He soon gave Adam and Eve the task of naming the animals. This sounds like a tough draw to me. I am not gifted with the ability to pick out the perfect name. Let's face it, I named my childhood dog Sniffee because he sniffed a lot.

They tell me that in the early church, priests got to give infants their Christian names, just before they immersed them in water for baptisms. I am still open to this practice making a comeback (the naming, not the dunking part). I would name everyone (boys and girls alike) for baseball players. I would use both first and last names. Our church would be full of Satchels, Madduxs, Hanks, Sandys, Willies, Christys, Mickeys, Morgans, and Babes.

My lone (and notable) exception to my inability for finding the perfect name concerns our (now-deceased) red fighting fish that I named "Ho Chi Fin." That one still feels brilliant.

When I found out my son Zec and his wife Sarah's second child was going to be a boy, I thought I might get in (yet another) request for a name. Perhaps this one would be perfect! My friend Mark

>>>--<<<

Turner's son Nick, who was our former student director, named his first son Asher *Mark* Turner, after his father; that seemed like a wonderful thing for a son to do. I figured even if Zec needed some help to think of it, this was a potentially great idea.

I had somewhat lobbied for *Shane* as a middle name for our first grandson, Maddox *Bishop* Blaha; as a first name for our second grandson, *Elijah* Christian Bishop; and as a middle name for our first granddaughter, Mabry *McKenna* Blaha – and was clearly 0-3. It is obvious to me now that I should have included cash incentives.

To make things easier for Zec and Sarah, I suggested the name *Shane Shane* Bishop, in hopes they would like either the first or the middle name. I truly didn't expect to get them both, but I often go to the table prepared to lose something, so I figured I was in perfect position to get either a first- or middle-name nod. Before the big moment arrived, Zec informed me that *Shane* had been ruled out as a first name, *Shane* had been ruled out as a middle name, and *Shane Shane* had been ruled out for the first and middle names both. I was reeling.

Zec informed me they were going with the name Isaac, which means laughter.

>>>--<<<

I told him if it was laughter they were going for, I am certain people would have laughed at *Shane Shane*.

P.S. It now seems clear that if anything is ever to be named for me, it will have to be a fish.

>>>--<<<

Discipline
(Fort Worth, Texas, circa 1969)

Dad is a southpaw. There are two files in my memory that verify this fact. One concerns the fact that I could never use his baseball glove. I could catch with it, but then I always threw like a girl. (These days girls throw really well, so I have no idea what I threw like.) The other concerns the position in which I was held, one fateful Sunday morning in Texas, to receive the discipline of the Lord.

It was 1969. I was seven years old. The *Miracle Mets* would win the World Series, the world was going crazy, and the Jesus Movement was just beginning to trickle into the Bible Belt from the coasts. Dad pastored a tiny Southern Baptist church outside Ft. Worth, Texas, where he also attended seminary full-time, and worked 40 hours a week stocking produce at the local Piggly Wiggly.

It was Sunday morning and the hymn selection was *Count Your Blessings.* As we began to sing something incredible happened; I interpreted it to be miraculous. A charismatic impulse fell upon me, though it apparently missed the rest of the congregation. (Not Baptist-bashing here; it can happen to anybody.) Compelled beyond any mortal

>>>--<<<

effort to resist, I jumped to a standing position on the top of my pew while the congregation remained seated. With great grace, poise and beauty, I began to count my blessings as I turned in 360-degree rotations. The jig began with one finger jutting into the air and with each rotation I would add an additional finger.

Though I was certain the rest of the congregation was richly blessed by the fact I had just invented Liturgical Dance, my dad apparently was not (being a fundamentalist and all). Somewhere between my fifth and sixth blessing (while my back was momentarily turned to the pulpit), something most unfortunate occurred: Dad darted from the pulpit, literally snatched me from the pew, tucked me under his left arm like a football, and shot down the aisle and out the back door like a running back rambling toward the end zone. The congregation kept on singing.

When we exited the sanctuary, he spun me from his left to his right side and began inflicting the discipline of the Lord upon my scrawny backside. I could still hear the congregation singing, *Count your blessings ...* **Smack** *... Name them one by one ...* **Smack** *... Count your blessings see what God hath done ...* **Smack.** (As to whether I was an inadvertent participant in the invention of percussion in worship is the topic of another story.)

>>>--<<<

After a brief and unbridled flurry of open-handed instruction, he stood me on my feet, glared at me, then ushered me into the church like a police officer ushers a convicted felon from a courtroom. The *cutting-edge* boy prophet of moments before was now paraded before the fickle assembly in absolute humiliation and returned to my mother on the front row. (Who was no doubt enjoying an escapist fantasy that I was the neighbor's kid and she had never seen me before.) Dad summarily returned to the pulpit, rechanneled his energy and preached a rather fiery sermon.

As I look back, that day taught me two lessons I will never forget. First: those on the cutting edge are often misunderstood by the masses, and second: the discipline of the Lord comes swiftly and from the left side.

>>>>> When I think of the prodigal son story, I see a father desperately trying to keep his family together. When one is in the other is out. There is drama and pain in this story. People can relate to that.
I can relate to that ...

>>>--<<<

Notes from a Trip to McDonald's, circa 2014

I took my three oldest grandkids to the McDonald's Playland for lunch today.

Here is the damage report:

1. Grandson one bitten by grandson two
2. Spilled drink
3. Granddaughter didn't want what she ordered and cried
4. Spilled drink number two
5. Granddaughter demanded that I scrape all the cheese off her cheeseburger
6. Granddaughter would not eat said burger because there were places where cheese was visible on the hamburger patty
7. In the Playland, Grandson one lost the gun to the plastic army tank that was his Happy Meal prize
8. Granddaughter would not leave because she made a new best friend
9. Grandson two lost his gun to his plastic tank.
10. No one really ate anything
11. Everyone cried when it was time to go

Summary: A better-than-average trip.

Can't wait until next week to do it again!

>>>--<<<

Nature is a classroom. Some of God's best students spend much time there.

Smoky Mountain Trees
(Great Smoky Mountain National Park, circa 2006)

There is no place in the world Melissa and I like to visit more than the Tennessee side of the Great Smoky Mountains National Park. Her people come from that area (and I wish mine did), so we both have a real link to the land and the people. We have been there dozens of times, and what we really love to do is day hike. We stay in really bad hotels (never stepping foot in Gatlinburg or Pigeon Forge), pack the SUV with iced Diet Pepsi, trail mix, Nature Valley Granola Bars and peanut butter and jelly sandwiches (which we call *trail steaks*).

Our adventures begin early as we find our selected trail head and set out for a day or part of a day. Melissa and I usually part company within a mile or two. She loves to push her body, get off the trail, forge ahead, and work through the pain of walking straight up a mountain. She is almost always bleeding somewhere after a hike. While she is a character in *Lord of the Rings*, desperately scaling Mt. Doom to dispose of the Ring of Power, I will sit at an overlook for half an hour eating a snack

>>>--<<<

and thinking, *Is God like six kinds of awesome or what?!*

Overlooking those blue, green mountains with their strands of mist hovering about them somehow fills my soul with peace. What I like best are the trees. In the Smokies you can't really tell where one tree begins and another ends, but the combined result is spectacular. The Great Smoky Mountains are an ocean of trees. A green, purple, blazing-red-and-yellow, misty ocean of trees.

Around our house in the Illinois suburbs of St. Louis, we have some really great trees located in old subdivisions or cemeteries. They are majestic and perfect! You might infer that the canopy of the Great Smokies consists of similarly perfect trees all lined up in a row, but you would have inferred wrongly.

As we hike, I sometimes pass by some trees that have been pushed down by a storm, and it always surprises me to see that none of them are perfect in any way. Where they enjoy sun exposure, they are well developed and gorgeous, but parts of every tree are stunted and deformed where the sun could not reach them. As I walk, nature reminds me that each tree has, in its own way, paid a price to be a part of something greater than itself.

>>>--<<<

I guess that is what being a part of the church is all about: Personal sacrifice to be a part of something greater than ourselves.

Getting Political (with Mabry)

Here recounts a political conversation I had with my 4-year-old granddaughter, Mabry:

Papa: Do like living in America?

Mabry: No.

Papa: What do you not like about America?

Mabry: Spiders. They are scary. I hate them.

Papa: The presidential candidates never mention spiders. They are clearly out of touch with the concerns of average Americans. Should Papa tell the candidates to get rid of American spiders because you are afraid of them?

Mabry: I am not afraid of spiders.

>>>--<<<

Reflections from The Fish Bowl No. 1

- Do the right thing the right way and you will get the right results in the right time.
- Everyone wants to change the world. Unless, of course, it requires something of them.
- Bad communicators make simple things complicated. Good communicators make complicated things simple.
- It is hard to think ahead when the roar of right now is deafening.
- When David saw Goliath, he ran toward him because the giant was an opportunity too big to miss!
- Blind ambition confuses position with purpose ... not all worthwhile things move up and to the right.
- There is nothing more difficult – or essential – than having to learn to work differently.
- When the kids are all throwing up their corn dogs, slow down the Scrambler.
- The U.S. American idea that leaders should not be expected to be role models is a stupid one.

>>>--<<<

My daughter Lydia shared a conversation she had with my granddaughter Mabry the other day. For me, it hits the wonder of grandchildren straight on.

The Tooth Fairy Revealed

Her brother Maddox had just lost a tooth that day, so the issue of the Tooth Fairy was clearly on Mabry's mind.

Mabry: So mom, are you the Tooth Fairy?
Lydia: Well, let me ask you some questions. Do you think there is someone whose job it is to keep track of all the kids who lose teeth?
Mabry: No.
Lydia: Do you think there is someone who sneaks into houses to take teeth and spends all her money to leave it under pillows?
Mabry: No.
Lydia: Do you think there is a place where mountains of baby teeth are hidden?
Mabry: No. (SILENCE)
So you are the Tooth Fairy?
Lydia: Now don't tell the other kids. They can find out when they are older. (SILENCE)
Mabry: So you *don't* work in St. Louis, do you?
Lydia: What?
Mabry: And you aren't in sales, are you?
Lydia: What?
Mabry: You are *THE* Tooth Fairy!

>>>--<<<

Later that evening at supper:

Mabry: Maddox, I have something to tell you.
Lydia: Mabry! You promised!
Mabry: It's about teeth ...

>>>>> When Melissa and I first got into ministry, people thought we were Ken and Barbie. Now they think we are Barbie and Barbie's Dad. <<<<<

Playing Christianity

I am convinced that most people know good and well the next step that God is calling them to make. And most often they don't make it because it is too small, not because it is too large!

I am convinced the reason God doesn't use very many people in significant ways is because they are unwilling to be obedient in insignificant ways. They are willing to do something "great" for God, but are unwilling to be faithful in the mundane. If we are going to be serious disciples of Jesus, we are simply going to have to do what he tells us to do.

At the end of the day we must ask, "Are we going to be obedient to God or not?" I know far more people who want to talk about obedience, discuss the dynamics of obedience, and study about Biblical examples of obedience than who are simply willing to be obedient!

Some spend their whole lives fussing with God. They want to serve God, but don't want to do what God is asking them to do. I remember when my son Zec was a little boy; he often wanted to help work in the yard, but he only wanted to help in the ways he wanted. I explained that when you *work* in the yard, you do what needs to be done. There is

>>>--<<<

another word that applies to doing what you what you want in the yard: *play*. A lot of people want to *play* Christianity but they don't want to *work* Christianity. Work requires obedience.

>>>--<<<

My paternal grandfather's name was Hallan Laverne Bishop. He died before I was born.
He named his only son Frederick Laverne Bishop. For some reason, Laverne II dropped the "e" and named his only son Shane Lavern Bishop (that is me).

They tell me that Laverne used to be either a guy's or a girl's name, but when the sitcom *Laverne and Shirley* hit the airwaves on ABC in 1976, it was all over. My middle name was toast.

In 1984, my son was born, and I felt the pressure of three generations of "Lavern(e)s" weighing heavily upon me.

He was screaming his lungs out, had a bluish tint, and his head looked like a peanut.
When the nurse came into get the name, Melissa and I responded in unison: "Zechariah Christian Bishop."

Sorry Laverne I and Laverne II;
Lavern III couldn't do it.

The kid seemed to have enough going against him already.

>>>--<<<

The Call (I Mean the Big One)
(Somewhere in West Tennessee, circa 1987)

I am often asked how a history teacher and coach raised by Jesus People became an ordained elder in the United Methodist Church. My first response is always that I have ruled out good luck. But upon serious reflection I was simply ... called.

In the spring of 1987 I was on a bus headed to the No Greater Love Ministries Mardi Gras Outreach. We were somewhere between the St. Louis Arch and the French Quarter when a voice inside my head simply said, "Go to seminary." That was it. No hints about which seminary, what I was to do with a seminary degree or what else might be involved; just a clear sense that God wanted something of me, and that I needed more training and seasoning.

These were the days before cell phones; when the next pit stop offered me the opportunity, I called Melissa from a pay phone and said, "Miss Anne, I can say without a doubt that God has called me into ministry. We are going to have to leave everything we know and go to seminary." She simply replied, "Okay." (She is awesome!)

Upon my return from New Orleans (and you *do* return), I applied for admission and scholarships,

>>>--<<<

called some district superintendents about a possible student pastorate, and by September, we were residing on Johnson Avenue in Manchester, Georgia; I was the pastor of the St. James-Manchester Charge. School had begun at Emory University and Melissa was holding our family of four together. It all happened that fast.

There have been many times since then that I have been discouraged in ministry, and a handful of times that I seriously thought about doing something else.

Then I remember my call (the big one); I did not enlist, I was drafted.

I can't quit.

Jesus called me and only He can release me.

You can't quit.

If you were called, only Jesus can release you.

Rev. Ralph Philippe was my associate pastor when I moved to Christ Church in 1997. No one ever lived more authentically in the fish bowl.

Reverend Ralph
(Jonesboro, Illinois, circa 1966)

My first associate pastor at Christ Church was Rev. Ralph Philippe. He was a retired Elder in the United Methodist Church and was our Pastor of Visitation. Ralph was impulsive, had a get-it-done gear like you wouldn't believe, and called it like he saw it. Ralph and I became fast friends; we ate lunch together about five days a week, and over the eight years we shared together in ministry, he served up many slices of his life. This was one of my favorites.

It was the summer of 1966, down in Jonesboro, Illinois, and Ralph was appointed to the Methodist Church there to begin his first post-seminary pastorate. That fall the church held a revival, and before the final service Ralph was informed of a family loosely affiliated with the congregation that was in dire financial straits. Ralph never was for hearing about a need and not acting upon it, so that evening Ralph put out an impassioned plea for the congregation to mobilize and help this family. To get things started they collected an offering. The following Sunday morning Ralph, did what no

Methodist pastor can do: he offered his resignation.

"People, last week I told you about a family in this community who needed the help of the church. We passed the plate and collected $33. I put in $20." Now his face was purple and his voice quivered, "I stand before you today to resign as your pastor, because I will not serve a church that refuses to help their own." Ralph left the sanctuary in the middle of the service, went home and started packing.

In Ralph's long and distinguished career as a United Methodist clergy person, there was only one short stay at a church. The Conference Journal simply reads, "Jonesboro. 1966."

>>>--<<<

I believe we exist for God; God doesn't exist for us.

I believe the question is never, "What can Jesus do for me?" but, "What can I do for Jesus?"

I believe God gives to us so we can give, not so we can have more.

I believe true happiness is found in submitting our desires to the desires of Christ for us.

I believe we become rich by giving, become great by serving and come alive by dying to self.

I believe I will never get a TV show.

>>>--<<<

Drawing God

When I was a boy, I liked to draw pictures of God. Especially during church (we didn't have smartphones back them). God was tall, middle aged, had a mane of white hair, and wore a black suit and thick glasses. I can't imagine why God needed glasses, but there they were. God wore glasses. If you didn't believe me, you could look at my picture for yourself. Even as a teenager, when I was once asked to draw God at camp, I drew the same guy. Every time.

Much later in my adult life, my mom explained that when I was very young we had a pastor who ... you guessed it, was tall, middle aged, white headed and wore glasses. She said I loved seeing him each week and was literally awed in his presence. For me, his face became the face of God. He just looked like God somehow ...

As I pondered this, I thought about how pastors uniquely represent God to children. Almost every week, children make me things, and I love taking a knee and talking to them on Sundays. Being a pastor through a child's eyes is both a joy and a sacred responsibility; it is one I do not take lightly. I am grateful for the almost 500 children who attend Christ Church each Sunday, and honored to

>>>--<<<

be seen as God's servant through their eyes! I am blessed and grateful. I pray I touch their young lives as profoundly as my childhood pastor touched my life!

>>>>> You should always promise less than you hope to deliver ... it is not a question of faith; it is a question of credibility.
What you do isn't the issue. It is whether you exceed or fail expectations.
The fish bowl hack is to always be lowering the expectations others place upon you ...
for the purpose of exceeding them! <<<<<

>>>--<<<

Are People Just Numbers (in a Mega-Church)?

Today I was informed that a beloved family of this church will be leaving us. Not because they are moving, but because they have lost a connection here and feel called to another congregation. It hurt.

I picked up the phone and called them, because I had some things I wanted to say. I wanted them to know what an honor it has been to speak into their lives over these years, and how grateful I am for their service here. I wanted to offer my blessing as they go, let them know they will be missed and let them know they need not hide if they ever run into me at a restaurant. I also offered to call their new pastor to say what an incredible family they are getting, if that would ever be of help.

I was thanked for calling and was glad that I did so. When I hung up, I wiped the tears from my eyes, took a short walk to compose myself and went back to work.

That is what I do, I go back to work.

So you think people are just numbers in a mega-church?

They are not to this pastor ...

Reflections from the Fish Bowl No. 2

- I would like to state for the record that I preach both steroid- and performance-enhancing-drug-free.
- If you are going to give God all the glory, let Him also carry all the stress.
- Sin is often found in the disconnection between our good intentions and our failure to act.
- Spiritual problems must be met with spiritual solutions.
- People want to change the world, not serve on committees.
- Worship. Serve. Repeat.
- To the tune of *Piano Man*. "It's 3 a.m. on a Saturday; I'm writing sermons again ... there's a computer sitting next to me ..."
- Evangelism is most difficult for those unsure of what they believe.
- What I never want to do as a theologian is to take the sins I am least dispositioned to commit and make them the worst.
- *Trendy* is not a synonym of *effective*.
- Jesus was always asking people to give up their religion and become a disciple.

I love the way my dad lives his life. He just goes for it, figuring he will have plenty of time to rest when he is dead.

Praise-a-Thons
(Herrin, Illinois, circa 1988)

For a while in the late '80s, Dad was active in Christian television. Active in the same sense piranha are active when they encounter blood. It was really a pretty good fit. Television loves larger-than-life personalities, and Fred Bishop is larger than several lives.

Dad loves to learn new things, and enjoyed getting to know the old pros from the Christian television circuit who took time to show him the ropes. For a while it seemed we could not turn on the television without seeing Dad. He did talk shows, he did remotes, he did panels and he did shorts.

When we would go to the mall, people would stop him and ask if he was the guy on television. It is not a difficult thing to be a celebrity in Southern Illinois. Like so many others, I watched, but not because I enjoyed the programming; I watched to keep an eye out for my dad. Excitement often gets the best of him.

>>>--<<<

Once a year, the regional station held a Praise-a-Thon. A Praise-a-Thon is like a telethon, only saved. For this event, national heavyweights would come to preach, croon and testify for the purpose of raising the station's annual budget.

My dad was a Praise-a-Thon machine. When money would roll in, it seemed to crank up his already heavily cranked metabolism. He would get downright giddy. At these times he would lose his perspective. Once he offered to personally deliver his hat to the next person to pledge. He and mom had to drive to Cape Girardeau, Missouri, to deliver the hat.

One year while Melissa and I were watching the Praise-a-Thon, money was coming in slowly. Impulsively, Dad decided to earn some of that money he wasn't being paid. He decided that for the next thirty minutes he would match the financial pledges of all callers to the station. I began to panic. Dad had no real money and I could imagine some millionaire calling in and pledging a few hundred thousand and hurtling Dad to debt and disgrace.

I did what any good son would.

I called the station. When they asked for my pledge, I informed them I was not calling to pledge. I told them I was Shane Bishop, Fred Bishop's son, my father had gone insane and I was calling to tie up the lines. I would neither pledge nor hang up. When they hung up on me, I immediately called back. The damage was manageable.

For years I couldn't understand how Dad could so lose his mind … then I came to Christ Church. We began to hold capital campaigns, and Melissa and I began to give more than we could have ever imagined. As we gave, God gave back to us and enabled us to give more.

It is a wonderful thing to get caught up in something bigger than you are. I am convinced true life happens at the precise point you become consumed in the stuff of God. Dad learned this long ago.

>>>--<<<

Peace, Be Still …

I was glancing over Facebook posts before bed tonight. Some people are mourning, some are crying out for justice, and others are lamenting the troubling state of world events. Each post offers testimony to the razor-thin line that separates order from chaos in our troubled existence.

For many it seems to be the end of the world.

At least the world as they know it.

Conversely, others were focused on St. Louis Cardinal baseball games, getting back to school, late-summer vacations, shedding a few pounds, sharing a new recipe, extolling a local restaurant, the newest movie, the upcoming football season, personal growth, pleasant weather, and relational drama. There is always relational drama.

For them it seems like just another day, but it is not just another day.

Today my burden is heavy. I wonder how to lead when I feel all the pain, but have no idea how to help. I wonder how I am going to sleep.

The writer of Ecclesiastes reminds us that in *all* times and in *all* seasons, God is still God. And with that realization, I lay my troubled mind on my pillow and pray for the Kingdom to come and come quickly; for justice to prevail, for love to defeat hate, and for peace to swallow violence whole.

And I pray, somehow, God might use my quivering voice to speak to a troubled region, nations and world and boldly say, "Peace, be still."

I spend a lot of time outdoors, where there are no parking lots, strip malls or people. There are, however, trees and mountains and streams. Nature calms my mind and spirit. To look at the intricate design of the physical world and think it happened by accident would be like throwing a stick of dynamite into a hardware store and the result being 27 perfectly designed and beautifully landscaped homes.

For me, nature is a bio-testimony to a creating God. It is a reminder that the God who created the world is also watching the world.

I think it takes more faith to be an atheist than a Christian.

Peace.

God is in control.

>>>--<<<

'Dear Pastor ...' (I Hate Those Letters)

This week I received a letter informing me that the writer wishes our church and its senior pastor took more stands on social issues and political positions. I get that, I really do.

As I was considering the content of the letter, something struck me. In a day and time when churches and denominations all across U.S. America are defining themselves by their stands on social issues, particularly issues around human sexuality, Jesus didn't do that at all ... ever. In fact, one of the great disappointments concerning Jesus in his own time was that in an Israel obsessed with the current reality of Roman occupation, Jesus didn't have a thing to say about the greatest political issue of his day. When they tried to force him to offer political commentary publicly, to speak to the issues of the day, he asked whose face was pressed upon on a silver coin and replied, "Give to Caesar what is Caesar's and give to God what is God's." I am guessing he got lots of letters.

Jesus flat-out refused to allow his culture to set his agenda. He simply did not spend his time teaching on politics or social issues; and had he done so, his central message would not have transcended his culture. The radical Jesus dealt exclusively with important things, often to the neglect of urgent things. Bigger things; often at the neglect of smaller things. Jesus dealt with things like hope, faith, love, hate, forgiveness, hypocrisy, truth and salvation. It was his genius.

Unlike modern religious culture today worldwide, Jesus never gave into the tyranny of the urgent.

I won't either. I believe when we deal faithfully with timeless things, those with an expiration date will find their proper place.

Technology and Church

What if Paul had refused to travel on those newfangled Roman roads?

What if Martin Luther had refused to use the printing press?

What if Billy Graham refused to use television?

What if the church today refuses to use the internet?

Reflections from the Fish Bowl No. 3

- If God has called you to Christian ministry, never forget you are in the people business. Otherwise you are just in business.
- To increase interest in the clergy as a vocation for young persons, I am advocating for both clergy action figures and trading cards.
- Just because people don't want the Gospel shoved down their throats, doesn't mean that people don't want the Gospel!
- Many churches today have become Holy Ghost-intolerant.
- When a church desires the presence of Christ above all else, they find they do not need anything else.
- There are people on Satan's payroll in most every congregation in America, and most of them would be horrified to know who is signing their checks.
- The Biblical idea of *lost* is much closer to "temporarily misplaced" than to "eternally doomed."
- The first question I ask prospective Christian leaders is, "Are you called?" The second is, "Do you have the stomach for this?"

Many of life's quiet lessons were taught to me by my mom. She has a certain courage about her…

Charles Wesley and My Mom
(Pinckneyville, Illinois, circa 1972)

The most important thing a church does is engage people in the worship of God, so it does not surprise me that conflict in churches historically centers upon the way we worship. Satan knows that if he can get churches expending energy debating worship styles, they will be all the less likely to actually worship.

In our own Methodist tradition, Charles Wesley was hotly criticized for bringing tavern music into the church as many of his hymns used popular English bar-hall melodies. Never mind they allowed non-church people to feel at home in the church because they knew the tunes, and never mind the Bible-based lyrics formed much of their initial exposure to theology. Never mind the Methodist movement transformed both England and America. Charles Wesley's methods were simply more than a good Anglican could stand, and that these tavern tunes would be played with so vulgar an instrument as a piano only exacerbated the tension.

>>>--<<<

Good Anglican Christians asked, "What is this world coming to?" Charles Wesley answered, "This world is coming to Christ!"

I remember the first time we did a chorus at the Oak Grove Baptist Church when I was a kid; I think it was the renegade song, *His Banner Over Me is Love*. I remember watching people cringe. After all, were we not singing a song accompanied by a guitar – the same instrument played by known drug user Jimmy Hendrix? Were we not participating blindly in what were quite possibly hand motions that may have been used in satanic rituals and other secret societies? Could anyone argue this song was to be found nowhere in the *Broadman Hymnal,* and thus was not cleared by God for use in church services?

Then I remember when my mom's high school all-girl singing group Joy covered Simon and Garfunkel's *Bridge over Troubled Water* in church before Dad preached. Troubled water indeed! Forget that the young people saw a connection between church, culture and everyday life for the first time. Forget that the lyrics had strong Christian implications and illustrated the text perfectly. Forget that our church was filling up with young people. The guardians of tradition were sure Joy would break into the Rolling Stones'

Satisfaction the next week, if something were not done and done right now.

Wesley was singing in 1772, freaking out the Anglicans, and my mom was singing in 1972, freaking out the Baptists; so it certainly appears that whatever controversy you may think is happening in the wide, wide world of church music, it is not new.

True movements of God historically occur when the Holy Spirit temporarily breaks loose from legalistic religious traditions, and they continue until a new set of legalistic religious traditions are constructed. Revival happens in the spaces between the way we have always done it and the way we will soon be doing it. Revival happens in the moments just after we lose control and just before we regain control again. Revival happens in short windows of opportunity, when God raises up courageous leaders to move us from what has always been to what soon will be. It takes courage to try new things and experiment with new expressions of worship; all the while holding fast to the unchanging Gospel message of Christ. To step out like that you need leaders.

Thanks Charles Wesley and thanks Jan Bishop for risking everything to connect people with Jesus Christ.

>>>--<<<

Twenty Core Values

Here are 20 core values that have propelled me to two effective decades of ministry at one church:

1. **Remember your call.** When things get tough, remember why you got into this.
2. **Keep your marriage strong.** If your marriage is bad, everything is bad.
3. **Stay in the Word.** Reading the Bible from cover to cover every other year or so is a great discipline.
4. **Keep learning.** Read. Attend conferences. Get a coach. Keep getting better.
5. **Never forget that you are in the people business.** You can't just sit in your office and be brilliant all the time. You have to add value to the lives of others.
6. **Don't take things personally.** Choosing not to get your feelings hurt is essential.
7. **Hold it steady.** Remember that God has you, your ministry and your family.
8. **Remember there are no shortcuts.** Realize you can't cheat the hours necessary for excellent work. Work smart. Work hard.
9. **Stay humble.** If God does bless your ministry, don't get all full of yourself. The second you get thinking you are all that and a bag of communion wafers, you are finished.

10. **Keep it real.** Just be an authentic human being who loves Jesus and who God called to lead. People can not only handle that, they will embrace it.

11. **Don't ignore problems.** Address them quickly.

12. **Tithe.** And give offerings on top of that.

13. **Hold on.** Remember that if God called you, you can't quit. He can release you, but you can't quit.

14. **Admit your mistakes.** You will make them. Offer forgiveness. Accept forgiveness.

15. **Choose peace.** Remember your detractors are not your enemies; they are your brothers and sisters in Christ.

16. **Determine your metrics.** Decide what a principled "win" looks like, and accumulate as many as possible.

17. **Take responsibility for everything.** If it is your fault, you can fix it.

18. **Take your vacations and your days off.** Take every single one of them. You are running a marathon, not a sprint. People will criticize you for it. Get over it.

19. **Do your job well.** Remember who signs your paycheck – that would be your local church – and give them your best time, effort, and energy.

20. **Have fun.** If you are not having a good time, no one else will be, either.

BAM!

Stop Apologizing for the Inexcusable

Imagine what might happen if the American church stopped trying to defend that of our history that is indefensible? What if we owned our collective sin and humbly asked God – and society– for forgiveness?

And what might happen if we Christians took it to the personal level and asked for forgiveness for our own failure to live a Christ-like life in front of our friends, co-workers and families? What if we actually admitted that we are sometimes hypocrites, we are often conflicted and we sometimes doubt and fear?

And what might happen if we Christians knocked the chip off our own shoulders, stopped arguing with everyone and actually started talking to people who may think differently than we? Not to convince them that we are right, but to truly attempt to understand, to hear, to feel.

And what might happen if I decided to listen before I spoke, attempted to show love and respect above all things, and broke free from my annoying addiction to having to be right ... on everything ... all the time?

Perhaps in this light of humility and love, the world may see the Light of the World in the church, in us, and dare I say, in me.

Imagine that!

>>>>> My dad reports that some years ago on an evangelism trip to the New Orleans Mardi Gras, the Spirit of God descended upon a street church.

There were 300 guys playing instruments and singing in the French Quarter and God showed up! The praise got so lively that the Baptists started shouting, the Pentecostals began to speak in tongues, the Presbyterians lifted their hands, and the Charismatics started dancing.

It was also reported that one of the Methodists got so excited that he took one of his hands out of his pocket. <<<<<

>>>--<<<

Future Prisoners of America
(Millstadt, Illinois, circa 2012)

In September 2011, Christ Church planted our first Campus about ten miles north of Fairview Heights, in suburban Maryville. We sent an incredible team of 50 bi-vocational ministers there to expand our ministries to two locations. By 2012, we had been called to start a second site, this one about 10 miles south of us in rural Millstadt.

On this day, some months before the Millstadt plant, Melissa and I were driving the town, attempting to get the lay of the land and see if God sparked something in our hearts for this community. After some scouting (which didn't take long), we stopped mid-afternoon at a pizza joint just off the main drag.

I expected we would be dining alone, but soon two or three beat-up pick-up trucks pulled up and in came a gaggle of rather rough looking, tattooed (and hickey-laden) twenty-something's (obviously gathering for a Future Prisoners of America Rally that was being held somewhere nearby).

Though the restaurant seating area was relatively spacious, they chose to sit at the table nearest to us, and soon all my ears could hear were their

>>>--<<<

braggadocios tales of fisticuffs, sexual conquests and abilities to consume alcohol in great quantities.

Gradually the conversation between Melissa and I ceased and my ear tuned into their conversations with digital quality. I began to consider the unfortunate reality that this particular group of young people would one day breed, producing yet more of their species.

When I couldn't take anymore, I said to Melissa – way too loudly – "I wish these punks would just shut up!"

And then it hit me, hard: If God was calling us to Millstadt, it was for these punks. If I could not love them, God would just have to send somebody there that could.

We planted our Millstadt Campus in September 2012.

A Prayer for Forgiveness

Almighty God,
Forgive your church, for we have stumbled and fallen in so many ways. Forgive your people, for we have failed to represent you well. Forgive me, for I am quick to speak and slow to listen; quick to judge and slow to understand. I am filled with pride and arrogance. Forgive us I pray, forgive me I pray, and free us through Jesus Christ our Lord.
Amen!

>>>--<<<

This was an epic fail. Not my first. Not my last.

God's Man of Power for the Hour
(Fairview Heights, Illinois, circa 1999)

I believe it happened in the springtime – sometime after Christmas and before Easter. I don't remember the specifics of the *when,* but I will never forget the *what* of this story.

I had been at Christ Church for almost two years and my ministry was just starting to get some traction.
A sense that God might have something really special for this congregation was just beginning to take shape in my heart.

In those days we had one worship service, and it started at 10:30 a.m.. We were one church, in one location, that met at one time. Those were great days. I arrived about 9:30 through the front glass doors, only to see a woman in a wheelchair out the corner of my eye. I did not recognize her, so I said a quick "hello" and went to my office to get things ready for church.

When I emerged about thirty minutes later, she was in the same spot, so I went to introduce myself. A quick glance verified that she was not in the chair to convalesce, but had been so confined for years and would be in that chair for the rest of her life.

As I approached her, something welled up within me. Something in my spirit said, "Reach out your hand and command her to walk." I had read about a similar instance in the Bible concerning Peter and John, and remember the encounter resulted in a once-lame man who went, "running and jumping and praising God."

In a split second I was right in front of her; would I obey God and set a miracle into motion, or would I miss God and make a scene that would embarrass the Lord (and his servant)?

At the moment of truth, I held out my hand and said (drum roll, please), "I'm glad you are here today."

With that, God's "man of power for the hour" walked into the sanctuary.

That scene has never been sponged from my memory. What if I had really heard the voice of God in that moment – and had obeyed it? What if she would have reached for my hand, received healing, and went, "running and leaping and praising God" throughout the narthex?

I will never know.

Over the years that scenario has never again presented itself in quite the same way. Perhaps I did the right thing. Perhaps I established that such a prompting was a waste of God's time.

I will never know. Tomorrow is another day …

>>>>> **You will be criticized no matter what you do. You will also be criticized if you do nothing at all. So do what is right. Do what is in your heart.** <<<<<

The Altar is the Other Direction
(Fairview Heights, Illinois, circa 1999)

Early in my stay at Christ Church, I asked our Associate Pastor, Ralph Philippe, to preach in my absence. Ralph preached on God setting us free from our addictions, and went out of his way to mention cigarettes. Ralph had been a hard-living construction worker before he met Jesus, and he had smoked like a chimney. He simply couldn't believe every Christian hadn't instantly given up every bad habit in their lives, because when Jesus found Ralph, he was delivered from his bad habits.

Apparently, as Ralph railed against Philip Morris and the good farmers of North Carolina, a (yet-to-be-delivered) parishioner could take it no longer. He stood from his pew, defiantly waved a pack of cigarettes at Ralph, and stormed out of the church mid-sermon.

Though I was out of town, my cell phone began to ring once the benediction was delivered. People just had to let me know what Ralph had done.

Later that afternoon I called Ralph to jokingly ask if it was impossible for me to be absent for even one week without him starting a riot. He just

>>>--<<<

chuckled. I asked him what he was thinking as the offended parishioner stormed out.

Ralph paused and replied, "I was going to tell him the altar was the other direction."

I really miss Ralph.

I had lunch with my mom. My thinning hair came up and I responded that I never thought it would happen to me, because Dad's hair still looks like it belongs on Moses.

Mom responded that such things normally come from the maternal line, to which I responded, "Did Grandpa Max have thin hair?"

She thought for a moment, "He had thick hair until he was in his mid-forties, and then it got very thin. Like yours really."

"Did he lose all of it?" I inquired. She said, "No, he died very young."

It was not a good lunch for genetics ...

>>>--<<<

Joining the Preacher
(Pass Christian, Mississippi, circa 1994)

A few years ago I would have told you I was a St. Louis Rams fan. In those years, the Rams were "the greatest show on turf." I watched all the games I could (I *do* work on Sundays), and thoroughly enjoyed the ride.

However, as the team began to break up (and later pack up), I discovered something shocking. I wasn't a Rams fan at all ... I was a Kurt Warner fan. My allegiance was to an individual player and not to the team. When Warner was traded to the New York Giants, I began to pay more attention to the Giants; by the time he landed with the Arizona Cardinals and had regained form, I followed that team closely.

Being a fan of a player rather than a team may not be a problem in sports, but it is a recipe for disaster when people are "joining the preacher and not the church."

Back when Kurt Warner was still stocking Hy-Vee grocery store shelves and before he was throwing touchdowns in the Arena Football League, a member of my Sumner congregation, Alvin Caldwell, attended the No Greater Love Mardi Gras Mission Trip. Early on that trip, several men attempting to get to know one another engaged in conversation under a huge tree at the Gospel Singers Camp, when someone asked Alvin, "Do you go to Shane's church?"

"No," Alvin replied. "Shane is the pastor at *my* church."

Four Minutes on the Appalachian Trail:

Dad: I want to walk on the Appalachian Trail.
Me: You are not feeling very well.
Dad: We don't have to go far.

Now on the trail at Newfoundland Gap in the Great Smoky Mountains National Park.

Me: Dad, remember that however far we go, we have to get back. Yell when you're at about half a tank.
Dad: I am there now.

We turn around.

Dad: I can still see the car.

>>>--<<<

Reflections from the Fish Bowl No. 4

- Here is something no preacher has ever said, "How will we handle the overflow crowds on Memorial Day weekend?"
- At Christ Church, we have VIP parking on Sundays for the senior pastor. It is in the shuttle lot about a quarter mile down the road; southwest lot, second slot from the driveway. I park there every week – unless of course someone is already parked there.
- Pastors need to stop expecting committees to do what God has called them to do.
- Seminary prepared me for a piano-, organ- and church-bulletin world. I graduated with honors in 1992, perfectly prepared to do ministry in 1958 ...
- Truth delivered without humility is still truth ... it just doesn't taste very good.
- Our task in ministry today is to hold fast to our theology and be flexible with our methodology.
- Success, wealth and privilege are far greater temptations to the church than marginalization, poverty and persecution.
- Our real problem with the Bible is not found in its ambiguity; it is found in its clarity.

>>> An End-of-the-Week Prayer <<<

I have given my all to you this week,
Almighty God, and I am tired. Thank you for the time of rest that awaits me.

Renew my strength, sharpen my mind
and soften my heart.

Give me thick skin, a quick smile and a heart
that sees the very best in everyone.

Give me strength to choose love over hate, justice over expedience and forgiveness over bitterness.

Keep a critical spirit from taking root in me, give me your boundless joy and help me remember to treat every person I see really well.

I am honored by your call upon my life, and humbled by how you have blessed me.

And don't worry, I'll be ready to go on Sunday.
Boy do I love Sundays! I'll bet you like Sundays, too!

In Jesus' name. Amen.

Lessons Learned

In some ways, this was the first real pastoral crisis of my pastoral ministry. There have been others since.

Dolly
(*Sumner, Illinois, circa 1994*)

I never will forget the Sunday morning Dolly walked into the Sumner church in the summer of 1994.

She was somewhere between 25 and 50 and wore stained clothing five sizes too small for her rotund body. Her fingernails were filthy, her hair was filthy and her feet were filthy. Dolly's acrid scent permeated the sanctuary. I would literally hold my breath to keep from gagging when I was within five feet of her.

Behind her trailed three ragamuffin urchins, resembling their mother in every way. Rodney was 10, Bill was 8 and Erica was 6. I sensed from the very beginning that God was keeping a careful eye on how we treated Dolly.

We were a growing, dynamic church containing the franchised, educated and powerful of the tiny community. Dolly would be a test for us all. I had no idea if we would pass or fail. No idea at all. Soon, Dolly, Rodney, Bill and Erica were regular fixtures at Sumner United Methodist Church.

The complaints poured into my office. Wherever Dolly chose to sit, the odor was so intense that people sitting around her became physically ill. Her two boys were whirling cyclones, prone to violence and shaped by a lifetime of neglect and abuse. When they would act up in church, Dolly would literally grab them by the ears and drag them out. She would seldom get to the back door before she would begin profanely swearing at the top of her lungs. A lot of good Methodists learned new words every Sunday.

We tried to help. We sent a work team to clean her house. The horrified team reported gaping holes in the flooring, no running water, animal feces, mountains of dishes and swarms of roaches eating various molding snack foods laying all over the disheveled house. We paid her water bill and brought in a used washing machine and hooked it up. We gave the family new clothes. Still, each week Dolly brought the children to church in filthy clothes, food caked to their faces and reeking of body odor. I don't ever recall seeing any of them in the clothes we gave them.

Neither church nor state could get Dolly to help herself or to improve the environment in which she was raising her children. And all the while I felt

>>>--<<<

God's piercing eyes upon us and heard Him saying that Dolly was His child and we had better treat her right.

One day, an unofficial spokesman came into my office and informed me that several of our families could bear it no longer; they were going to leave the church. They were truly sorry, exasperated, out of ideas and could take no more of Dolly. These were good families. They gave their offerings each week, came every Sunday morning and evening and helped where needed. Their absence would be devastating to the congregation.

There was not one point brought before me with which I disagreed. Dolly smelled, she shouldn't have those children, she was abusive, her home was a pigsty, her kids were disruptive and the church was in chaos the moment they stepped in the door. She and those kids would never contribute a dime, had cost us a fortune and were driving off the very people who tried to help her.

Yet there was Dolly, created from the dust in the image of God, with all that dust and more still on her. Something inside her troubled mind told her that her family needed to be in church and they attended each Sunday oblivious of the tsunami they were causing.

>>>--<<<

I told the spokesman to tell his people to do what they had to do, but Dolly and her children would be welcomed as long as I was the pastor. But before they quit the church *en masse*, I asked them to read James 2:1-13 and let me know what they thought.

When the people read James' thoughts on the poor and that there will be no mercy for us if we are unmerciful to others, they were cut to the heart (the way good Christians often are). No one quit the church, and Dolly was welcomed each week.

But problems like Dolly and her family normally come with a shelf life.

Within a year and a half, both bill collectors and the Department of Children and Family Services were growing impatient; she had burned most of the bridges people of good will had extended to her. One day, she took her children, loaded them into a car that barely ran and left town. She left bills unpaid and the shack to the roaches and dogs. She left the filthy clothes where they lay and the clean clothes we gave her folded in a pile and she didn't look back. She didn't need a moving van; the television fit in the trunk, and little else was worth taking.

Dolly was gone as quickly as she had come. I must

confess there was a sense of relief for me. It was the kind of relief you feel when you turn in a final exam over material you barely understood and though you didn't ace it, you know that you passed.

We had done well, for in welcoming Dolly, we had welcomed Christ.

Dolly never returned.

>>>--<<<

This story illustrates how God uses even "weapons formed against us" to make us better. Only God can turn a curse into a blessing!

Backhanded Compliments
(Carterville, Illinois, circa 1982)

I have a photograph of the 1982 men's tennis team of John A. Logan College. I am the guy square in the middle with the brand-new Prince Pro racquet, Peter Frampton hairdo and fashionably short shorts. You can't miss me.

DuQuoin High School did not have a tennis team, so I walked on and made the college squad, having never had a single lesson or played in a formal match. Most the other guys had beautiful ground strokes, powerful serves and well-orchestrated footwork. All I had was quickness and speed from playing lots of tennis at the City Park and what I had learned from Tennis Magazine.

My main weapon was treachery. I played number five singles, and never met a single opponent who wasn't a better tennis player than me. Early in the match, I would determine the player's primary weakness (number five players always have a weakness), then spend the rest of the afternoon exploiting it. I won far more than I should have.

>>>--<<<

When we would practice, Coach Bechtal would always have me spar with the better players, and I never could figure out why. Then one day he explained things to me: In consistently exposing and relentlessly attacking our top players at their point of weakness, by me trying to defeat them, I actually made them better! He explained that although I would never get much better (that hurt), my greatest contribution to our team was not my .500 record as a number five singles player; it was incrementally helping our top players improve by trying to defeat them!

Are there some challenges in front of you today? Do they seem overwhelming?

Rather than allow them to defeat you, see them as things God will use to make you better, stronger and better fit for his service!

Isn't it amazing how things designed to beat you can actually make you better?

>>>--<<<

Forgetting to Remember
(Fairview Heights, Illinois, circa 2009)

I had a really bad day. Nothing really went wrong, but I couldn't find the hours to accomplish what I needed to do. As the day wore on and deadlines approached, my mood became worse and worse. By late afternoon I had clearly deteriorated from affably ineffective to generally curmudgeoned.

I had run my emotional gas tank dry at the office; now I was about to come home with no fuel left in the tank. As I pulled into our driveway and walked into the kitchen, I brought my bad mood along with me (I should have left it at church). It was clear Melissa had enough of the both of us after about three minutes. My daughter Lydia was over, and she just stayed out of my way.

As I generally stormed about the house feeling like a caged tiger, I suddenly noticed my baby grandson Maddox in the living room. He was lying on a blanket on the floor, and he stopped me in my tracks. I plopped down beside him. He is so cool. He looks like all the other blondes in our tribe, has dimples like me and his hair sticks straight up. One day he is going to learn to switch hit, knock down fifteen-foot jump shots and become a mighty man of God. Suddenly all those things I needed to do didn't seem quite so important anymore. My bad mood just seemed selfish and silly.

As I looked at him, I was reminded of the goodness of God. I thought about how blessed I am to have an incredible wife to share my life, a beautiful family, good health and a great church to serve. How could someone so blessed get so bent out of shape over so little? Sometimes we forget to remember God's blessings. I forgot for a while, but Maddox helped me remember.

>>>>> **It was not until my early thirties that I discovered sarcasm is not a spiritual gift. Sarcasm is just anger with a sense of humor.**
It stings. It hurts others. It is not funny.
I get that now.... Usually.<<<<<

>>>--<<<

Early Marriage Story No. 1
(DuQuoin, Illinois, circa 1984)

Melissa and I married young. She was nineteen going on thirty-seven and I was twenty going on twelve-and-a-half.

Despite our disparate maturity levels, Melissa had learned little about some of the basics of living. We were married almost a year before I discovered that she threw our bank statements and cancelled checks away with the junk mail. Thinking back, it is clear that we had failed to negotiate responsibilities around the house. I used my parent's (Leave-it-to-Beaver-style) arrangement as a default, but since she grew up in a single-parent household, she had no template at all. We both had a few holes.

Fresh out of college with a newly minted teaching certificate in hand, I had a job interview coming up and had picked out my favorite outfit to wear. My "go-to" outfit in those days was a button-down light blue shirt and a pair of Levi's Dockers. Not too casual, not too stuffy. Sweet!

For some odd reason, I assumed Melissa knew how to do the laundry and the ironing. And since my mom was particularly skilled in this area, I had high expectations. Come to find out, no one had ever taught Melissa how to iron, but to her credit, she did the best she could, and when my favorite brownish-tan khakis were laid out for me to wear, there were two crisp creases … both on the left leg.

This would be a sensitive situation for even a mature person, but that description had little to do with me. Thinking I was hilarious, I quipped "Melissa, most people only wear one crease per leg."

I don't remember her response at all, but what I can tell you is we celebrated our 34th wedding anniversary on May 21, 2017, and she has never again ironed a single thing for me in all those years. Nothing.

On the one or two occasions I have asked her to do so, she responds, "No one likes to do nice things for complainers."

It doesn't seem so hilarious now.

I call this unfortunate event early marriage "Tactical Error No. 1."

Lessons Learned No. 1

- We are all full of something, and we all leak.
- Something is always chasing you. Calamity pursues the evil and blessing pursues the righteous.
- I am a card-carrying member of the Dairy Queen Blizzard Fan Club ... deal with it.
- I was going to wait to write until there was significant demand for my material, and then I noticed I wasn't getting any younger ...
- Why is it that updating to newer technology always means things I used to know how to work, I don't know how to work anymore?
- Having a great attitude does not guarantee a great day, but it will up your odds exponentially!
- I took a Dave Ramsey course ... not going to set up a budget, but I did buy a blue shirt ... in cash.
- Some of the most un-Christian things ever to happen on this planet have been done in the name of Christ. It is inexcusable.
- When you fall down, get back up! That being said, you might want to grab a quick nap first.
- It is no longer an expert's world; it is a learner's world.
- Take responsibility for everything that goes wrong in your world – everything! If it is your fault, you can fix it.

>>>--<<<

Early Marriage Story No. 2
(Louisville, Illinois, circa 1985)

I had landed a job teaching and coaching at the junior high school of North Clay Unit 25, immediately upon my graduation from Southern Illinois University at Carbondale. I taught seventh- and eighth-grade American History and coached baseball and basketball. My teaching job paid about $12,000 each and every year, and coaching drove my annual salary up to $14,000. Even in 1985 that was not a lot of money.

Melissa and I had already decided she would stay home with our infant son Zec, so I was the proverbial bread winner – and was clearly a few slices short of a loaf. When summer came around, I was clearly in the market for a summer job and quickly found one at the Epworth Campground just out of town. My job was an interesting one. When kids were not in camp, I was to mow and do general maintenance, and when camp was in session, I played my guitar, sang and taught classes. But most of that summer, I went to work with no shirt, a pair of overalls, and a Toronto Blue Jay's baseball cap and returned home each evening a sweaty, sunburned mess.

On my first day, camp president Phil Poe asked if I knew how to operate a tractor and mower. I told

>>>--<<<

him I was raised in Southern Illinois and we both laughed. What I neglected to tell him was that I was raised at on North Line Street in DuQuoin, and had never been on a tractor in my life.

When I arrived alone at the shed, I climbed aboard the mower and looked fervently for the key to turn the ignition and for the accelerator. Finally, I walked back into town and found a guy who showed me how to operate the tractor and mower – after making me feel like an idiot for 45 minutes. All in all it was a fair trade.

Later in the summer, a water line broke underground, and Phil asked if I knew how to dig it up and fix it. I again told him I was raised in Southern Illinois, and we both laughed (that one also resulted in a walk into town).

Since we only had one car (a 1969 Pontiac LeMans someone had given us), Melissa and Zec drove me to work each morning, brought me lunch at noon and picked me up at the end of each day. During one particularly hot stretch of weather, the camp was abandoned except for me, the tractor and the mower. I remember the morning being hotter than six kinds of smoke, and all I could think about was the Coca-Cola poured over ice that Melissa would soon bring me. I was counting the minutes. When I saw that powder-blue muscle car rolling up the

>>>--<<<

dust, I was crazy excited. Melissa got out of the car and had everything on a tray for me. I spotted a sandwich, some chips and a cookie (blah, blah, blah) and then ... there it was! Perched majestically and towering over the tray was my glass bottle of Coca-Cola. I raced the tractor over to the car, imagining I was Charles Ingalls from *Little House on the Prairie*, getting ready to have a big meal after chopping wood to keep his family warm or having saved his milk cow's newborn calf.

Melissa looked so happy to present her picnic plate to me and I thanked her profusely ... almost. Right when I was about to shower her with thanks, I noticed there was no ... ice. She had not brought ice. There is no way words could possibly describe my disappointment. What was intended to be a gracious, "Thank you, sweetheart!" came out as a terse, "Where is the ice?"

Melissa summarily put the tray on the ground behind the back tire, then got in the car and floored the accelerator, leaving the lunch tray underneath roughly six inches of dust. Only the neck of the lukewarm Coke bottle was visible to the naked eye. I watched the dust roll until the car was out of sight, in utter disbelief of what had just happened.

This unfortunate event I call "Tactical Marriage Error No. 2".

This story literally changed my life, my ministry and my career. I owe much to Harold.

Harold
(*Sumner, Illinois, circa 1994*)

Harold killed people in World War II, and then worked 30 years in a condom factory. These two life events shaped his personality like an irregular pair of shoes eventually deforms the feet.

Harold was my neighbor. I walked by his mobile home each day on my way to and from the parsonage and the Sumner United Methodist Church.

I was warned about Harold: "He is a recalcitrant, and curmudgeon old man who doesn't like anybody, but especially hates preachers." Harold sat outside in good weather and I cheerfully greeted him every morning and evening. He raised a hand but never spoke. This was our routine and we did it every day.

One day, he said, "I heard you like sweet tea."

I replied, "That is not exactly right; I like fresh-brewed, southern sweet tea, where the sugar is melted in while the water is hot."

>>>--<<<

He said, "I can make tea like that. Stop by sometime." I told him I would, and walked on to work (we had been at this for three years; I didn't want to appear easy.)

A couple of weeks later I paid Harold a call, and he talked about World War II. He spoke of young men who didn't return home, described the face of a female German sniper he had shot out of a tree, described the circumstances that resulted in him receiving two Purple Hearts, and of watching his own surgery being performed in the chandelier above him.

He also spoke of how badly the church had hurt him as a young man, and he cried through most of it. He then turned off the tears, said he didn't need me or the church and I was curtly dismissed. I left a half glass of sweet tea on his table.

After that our relationship returned to normal, but I thought a lot about Harold.

One night his wife Edna called me in the early morning hours, in a panic. "I can't control Harold; he is having seizures and the ambulance isn't here. Can you come and help me?"

>>>--<<<

When I arrived, Harold was in the restroom with his eyes rolled back in his head, pants hanging at his ankles, and he was urinating all over the place as he convulsed against the wall. I took a deep breath, waded in and helped Edna. All the while Harold was crying out to God. "God, if you will let me live, I will give my life to you."

The ambulance arrived, strapped Harold to a board and took off for Evansville, Indiana. I went home and took a really long, really hot shower, threw my clothes in the washing machine and went to bed.

A couple of days later, I drove the hour-and-a-half to Evansville and entered Harold's room. He was in pretty bad shape, but that did not keep him from literally turning away from me. We sat in silence for several minutes. When Harold saw I wasn't going to leave, he whispered over the oxygen tank, "I meant what I said about giving my life to God; I meant that. But you won't be seeing me in your church. I am going to watch Robert Schuler on television."

For some reason, that really hacked me off, so I got about two inches from the tube that was up Harold's nose. "I have a great idea for you Harold; the next time you are having seizures, peeing all over the restroom, and are about three-quarters nuts, why don't you have Edna give Robert

>>>--<<<

Schuler a call? See if he will get out of bed and come over to your house in the middle of night, help your wife care for you and endure your unique physiological rendition of showers of blessing?"

I slammed the hospital door behind me and left. It occurred to me this was possibly not a textbook example of pastoral care. There would be no case study.

Harold was released the next week, and though he never said a single thing about our hospital conversation, he also never missed another worship service at the Sumner United Methodist Church. He sat about midway back and to my right. Edna sat next to him, beaming. Harold was alive and in church; her prayers had been answered.

About a year later, I received another call from Edna. Harold was dead in his La-Z-Boy, and she wondered if I would stop by and sit with her until the coroner arrived. There we sat in three chairs in the tiny living room; Edna, Harold and me.

Edna began to cry, "I don't exactly know what you said to Harold in the hospital room, but it changed his life."

>>>--<<<

A bit perplexed, I asked, "Did Harold say anything at all about our conversation?"

Edna replied, "Not really; he just said you were the first preacher who ever explained things to him in a way he could understand."

Looking back, I did almost everything wrong. I certainly would not have made my Pastoral Care professors in seminary proud. But I learned something: God can bless almost anything … even a really bad hospital visit. Yes, God can bless anything but nothing. I determined long ago to always give God something to bless. Harold taught me that.

Lessons Learned No. 2

- I figure we are all crazy ... the only question is one of degrees. I just want to be God's kind of crazy.
- Sometimes you have to shove on some things just to see if they will move.
- Many people are wrong. Few are uncertain.
- I want "Bacon's" agent. If unavailable, get me "Avocado's or "Pistachio's."
- I was going to play in the water with the grandkids today, but we got rained out ...
- An e-mail I just read ended with these words, "Save the Earth, it's the only planet with chocolate."
- I am often tempted to add Spanish as a "language I know" on my profile, but then reality hits me ... I speak Spanish like Tarzan spoke English.
- Being on vacation while staying home is like retirement practice.
- Leading a church in this new world is like walking through a Midwestern cow pasture. No matter how hard you try, it is hard not to step in something.

>>> Use Me Lord (Please) <<<

Almighty God, strengthen in me all that is good, noble and Christ-like.

Break the grip of all things vain, cowardly and selfish.

Forgive me for trusting too little, worrying too much and not loving enough.

Use me today in some unexpected way. Whether it be significant or seemingly trivial, use me for your glory.

Touch a life through me. And when I go to bed tonight, give me the grace to know I have truly lived on this day.

In the strong name of Jesus ...
Amen

The Happy Ending

As I get older, I can't but notice my conceptualization of life is changing. Life has become a precious thing; something not to be taken for granted. Life's finitude is clearly exacerbated by the ever-increasing speed of the game. And there is a little less of life left each day; like the most delicious steak you have ever eaten getting smaller one bite at a time on one hand, while each bite is more appreciated on the other.

As I pile on city, off-road, and highway miles alike, I am less inclined to try to figure everything out or to demand to know, and more inclined to behold, enjoy and appreciate.

I simply do not have an overriding need for the world to make sense or to be the smartest person in the room these days. That is convenient, because I am obviously not as smart as I once thought I was. At first that particular epiphany hurt a bit, but now, it seems freeing. I am happy to leave that illusion with the person in the room who most needs it.

I have never known less.

I have never had less to prove.

>>>--<<<

I have never been happier.

I will close with a blog I posted earlier this summer. It seemed incredibly unexceptional when I released it, but within a couple of months, it had exceeded 2 1/2 million reads worldwide, and continues to churn to this day.

The article dealt with happiness, and convinced me of three very profound things:

1. People want to be happy
2. People have no idea how to be happy
3. People are willing to read blogs about happiness

We started our journey with death; let's end with life. Better yet, with happiness! Here is the blog:

Twelve Things I See Happy People Do (That Unhappy People Do Not)

I have been thinking a lot about happiness of late, partially because so many people seem unhappy. I think that was my first epiphany upon entering the world of social media: people are unhappy and there are a lot of them.

Now don't get me wrong; we all know some people who wouldn't be happy, were they not unhappy, but I am not talking about them. We will just let them be. I am also not thinking theologically here (i.e., juxtaposing happiness and joy). Instead, today I am going to err on the practical and pragmatic side of things.

With that being said, let's get going.

I think most people want to be happy; they are just not quite sure how to get there from their present location. I believe the best route to happiness is found by following the footsteps of those who have already arrived. Here are my thoughts on the topic that have been formed by watching happy people:

>>>--<<<

1. Focus on what you have (not what you don't).

Unhappy people are unthankful people. The practice of counting your blessings is a great start. Get out a legal pad and write down all the good things in your life. Often unhappiness sneaks in when we lose sight of all the good things in our life and become focused on one or two difficult things.

2. Question the sources of your expectations.

Most unhappy people want things they don't have … and they want them bad. Are these expectations realistic? Who is selling them to you? I hope not the media. Having a miserable existence because you are not living into a pipe dream is really tragic.

3. Be Generous.

Study after study has come to the same conclusion: Selfish people are miserable. Happy people give of their time and resources to a cause greater than themselves.

4. Remember happiness is not a destination.

The happiest people I know are those least conscious of their own happiness. Happiness is learning to enjoy the ride, not reaching your destination.

5. **If you don't like your life, change it.**

Take control of your own life. Do you want to learn to play the piano? Take lessons! Do you regret not getting a college degree? Get one. Do you want to improve your spiritual life? Start going to church. There is really no one holding you back but you.

6. **Slow down.**

You just can't smell the roses at a full sprint! If you, like me, are a workaholic type, build time into your Outlook calendar to do nothing. Get a hobby. Enjoy your friends and family. Happy people have learned how to occasionally chill.

7. **Realize there are no shortcuts.**

If you were honestly disappointed you didn't win the billion dollar Power Ball, you are not getting it. Getting your education, working hard, putting in the hours, pursuing your dreams, saving and giving are always in style.

8. **Stop feeling entitled.**

No one owes you anything. Just assume you are not going to get any help, you will receive no inheritance and that no one is going to give you a break. Now go make your life happen! If anything else comes (and it probably will), it is all bonus!

9. **Think significance.**

Significance is achieved by leaving the world better than you found it. People who feel their lives really matter are the happiest people of all!

10. **Forgive.**

Forgiving those who have hurt you breaks their power over you. Forgiving yourself for your failures frees you for future success. Ask God to forgive you. Ask those you have hurt to forgive you. Make restitution where you can. Move on.

11. **Remember, a great attitude is a choice, not a disposition.**

We can control our feelings or we can be controlled by them. Happy people *choose* to have great attitudes.

12. **Speak life.**

When you speak, choose words that uplift, encourage and bring positive energy into every situation. My mom was right, "If you don't have something nice to say, you shouldn't say anything at all." People who speak life are like human air fresheners.

Tomorrow morning when you awaken, you have an opportunity to invest in your own happiness, or to make yourself miserable. If you choose the former, you will make others happy as well.

If you choose the latter … well, you know.

>>>--<<<

I think the key thing to remember when you write is that you are hoping to add value to the lives of others.

It is not about you, it is about them.

It is not about how you feel, it is about how you make them feel.

No writer is all that interesting, and no story is truly unique, but if our stories connect others to their own stories and open up their hearts, we have done something of great value.

I hope this book added some value to your life.

I hope it eased your pain, brought healing, equipped, encouraged,
and inspired you in some way.

And it even had a happy ending!

Happiness ... now there is an elusive topic.

I wish someone would write a book on that!

Hmmm ...

About the Author
Shane L. Bishop

Rev. Shane L. Bishop has been the Senior Pastor at Christ Church in Fairview Heights, Illinois, since 1997. In 2010, Shane was named a Distinguished Evangelist of the United Methodist Church by the Foundation for Evangelism. With his strengths of vision casting, preaching and leadership, weekend worship attendance has increased from approximately 200 in 1996 to over 2,300 in 2017. Christ Church has been recognized many times as one of the fastest growing United Methodist Churches in America, and the Illinois Great River Annual Conference has recognized Christ Church 12 times with the Award for Church Growth and Evangelism.

A former history teacher and coach, Shane holds both graduate and undergraduate degrees from Southern Illinois University-Carbondale. An Elder in the Illinois Great Rivers Conference, Shane graduated *cum laude* in 1992 from Candler School of Theology at Emory University. There, he received the Rollins Scholarship Award for his academic work and effectiveness in pastoral leadership at the St. James-Manchester Charge in Manchester, Georgia. From 1992-1997 he served the rural Sumner/Beulah Charge in Sumner, Illinois, where he was presented the Denman

>>>--<<<

Evangelism Award in 1994 before being appointed to Christ Church.

Elected to represent the Illinois Great Rivers Conference at General Conference three times and Jurisdictional Conference four times, Shane has traveled extensively in ministry around the country and the world. Shane's first book, *Exactly As I Remember It,* was released in 2012 and his second book, *Re:Member,* in 2013.

Shane resides in Belleville, Illinois, with his wife of thirty-four years, Melissa. The couple have two adult children and four grandchildren. He enjoys blogging, reading, history, the St. Louis Cardinals, the Smoky Mountains and being a Papa.

Shane hopes to be remembered as someone who loved God, loved people and didn't do dumb crap.